Armageddon's Glorious End

David Manzano

TEACH Services, Inc.
P U B L I S H I N G
www.TEACHServices.com • (800) 367-1844

World rights reserved. This book or any portion thereof may not be copied or reproduced in any form or manner whatever, except as provided by law, without the written permission of the publisher, except by a reviewer who may quote brief passages in a review.

The author assumes full responsibility for the accuracy of all facts and quotations as cited in this book. The opinions expressed in this book are the author's personal views and interpretations, and do not necessarily reflect those of the publisher.

This book is provided with the understanding that the publisher is not engaged in giving spiritual, legal, medical, or other professional advice. If authoritative advice is needed, the reader should seek the counsel of a competent professional.

Copyright © 2017 David Manzano
Copyright © 2017 TEACH Services, Inc.
ISBN-13: 978-1-4796-0826-3 (Paperback)
ISBN-13: 978-1-4796-0827-0 (ePub)
ISBN-13: 978-1-4796-0828-7 (Mobi)
Library of Congress Control Number: 2017916369

Scripture quotations marked The Message are taken from The Message. Copyright © 1993, 1994, 1995, 1996, 2000, 2001, 2002. Used by permission of NavPress Publishing Group.

Scripture quotations marked NASB are taken from the New American Standard Bible®, copyright © 1960, 1962, 1963, 1968, 1971, 1972, 1973, 1975, 1977, 1995 by The Lockman Foundation. Used by permission.

Scripture quotations marked NIV are taken from The Holy Bible, New International Version®, NIV®. Copyright © 1973, 1978, 1984, 2011 by Biblica, Inc.™ Used by permission. All rights reserved worldwide.

Texts credited to NKJV are taken from the New King James Version®. Copyright © 1982 by Thomas Nelson, Inc. Used by permission. All rights reserved.

Scripture quotations marked NLT are taken from the Holy Bible, New Living Translation, copyright © 1996, 2004, 2007 by Tyndale House Foundation. Used by permission of Tyndale House Publishers, Inc., Carol Stream, Illinois 60188. All rights reserved.

Scripture quotations marked REB are taken from The Revised English Bible, copyright © Cambridge University Press and Oxford University Press 1989. All rights reserved.

Table of Contents

Revelation—The Last Book in The Bible: "Is It Important?" . 5

Why This Book? 11

Why Do We Believe? 15

Revelation—Christ's Book of Victory. 19

Making Sense Out of The Existence of Satan 23

The Christ of Revelation 29

Revelation's Unity and Order of Events. 35

Symbols in the Visions of Revelation 39

The Number 7 in the Book of Revelation 41

The Seven Churches 43

The War Against Christ's Church and His Gospel 45

The Seven Seals Portray Christianity 53

God's Sealing Work (Revelation 7:1–3) 57

The Seven Trumpets 61

Heaven's Warning Message to Earth (Revelation 10) 65

Light from God's Temple in Heaven 71

The Prominence of the Temple of God in the Book of Revelation 77

A Woman, Her Child and the Dragon (Revelation 12) 79

Revelation 13, Two Beasts and the Mark 83

The Mark of the Beast 87

Revelation 14 91

What the Three Angels of Revelation 14 Tell Us 95

Babylon in the Book of Revelation. Revelation 14:8 97

Armageddon 103

Seven Last Plagues (Revelation 15 and 16) 109

Babylon Judged (Revelation 17 and 18) 113

Victory! (Revelation 19) 117

The Millenium (Revelation 20) 121

The New Jerusalem (Revelation 21 and 22) 125

The Bride, The Lamb's Wife 127

John's Story — Revelation as Narrative 131

Appendix 137

Bibliography 207

Revelation — The Last Book in The Bible: "Is It Important?"

Seals and trumpets; monstrous beasts; the "mark"; destruction and a re-created earth. These are many of the elements in the biblical book of Revelation. How shall we look at this book? Some say, "It can make you weird or wacko," or "It is not needed today. It was to give encouragement to Christians in the first century."

"The Revelation of Jesus Christ which God gave to Him," is how the book begins. The importance of this book is indicated in several ways.

First, it is the work of the Godhead—the Father, Son, and Holy Spirit; and also angels. All were involved in the giving of this book. God the Father gave it to Jesus.

Christ appeared to John and told him to write in a book the things he saw. John was in the Spirit. The Spirit moved upon John, enabling him to see, hear, and write the visions presented to him. The Spirit and angels spoke to John (see Rev. 1:1, 10–18; 2:7, 11, 17, 29; 22:16).

A second indication of the importance of Revelation are the words of verse 3. A blessing is pronounced on those who "read, hear, and keep the things that are written in this book." The blessing is for "whoever has ears to hear" (13:9). The blessing, with an added warning, is repeated as the visions end (see Rev. 22:7).

Jesus said, "I have told you before it comes to pass, that when it comes to pass you might believe" (John 14:29). The events portrayed in Revelation begin with the time of John and go through Christian history to the time when the New Jerusalem comes down from God, all things are made new, and His people are forever with Him (see Rev. 21).

Many of its prophecies have occurred. As we see them unfold through history, our faith strengthens. As we see God's plan of salvation moving to its climax, we discover our position in it. Strength and security come with the knowledge of God's prophetic truth. Prophecy is a "light shining in the darkness." Its light brings one close to Christ (2 Peter 1:19). There is a great blessing contained in the book of Revelation.

Another, more striking indication of the importance of Revelation is the prominence of the gospel in the book. There are those who ask, "What has Revelation got to do with the gospel? It is the gospel that is important." They are right. It is the gospel that is important.

Revelation presents the "everlasting gospel" in all its completeness. It speaks of the time when "the mystery of God should be finished." It announces "the hour of God's judgment is come," and when God says, "It is done" (10:7; 14:7; 16:17). It portrays earth's harvest and the day when the problem of sin has been completely settled, thus fulfilling the purpose of the gospel of our Lord Jesus Christ.

The prominence of the gospel is evident as the book begins. The book comes from Jesus Christ, the name with which John was familiar; the name which all Christians knew and trusted; the name which speaks of His birth and life on earth. "He lived among us." John breaks into a doxology to the world's Savior: "To Him who loves us and washed us from our sins by His blood. He has made us to be a kingdom, priests to His God and His Father. To Him be glory and dominion forever" (Rev. 1:5, 6).

The gospel is evident in the twenty-eight times in which Jesus is referred to as "the Lamb" [It was when Jesus was baptized that John the Baptist introduced Jesus as "the Lamb of God" (John 1:29)]. The first Lamb reference in Revelation is 5:6, where John saw in the middle of God's throne "a lamb standing as if it had been slain." The twenty-four elders sing to the Lamb saying, "You are worthy, for You were slain, and have redeemed us by Your blood." Every time Jesus is called the Lamb, it is a reminder of His sacrifice that made our salvation possible.

Chapters 4 and 5 reveal that the Lamb controls the outcome of earth's history. Every action decreed from the throne of God is made in light of and reference to "the Lamb that was slain." It is the climax of the "everlasting gospel" that is presented in Revelation 14:6–20. In Revelation 19, John saw Jesus riding forth in all His glory and majesty. All the armies of heaven follow Him. What garment does Christ wear? John saw the robe Christ wears. It is a "robe dipped in blood" (19:13).

The blood of Christ is the emblem of His victory. "As often as you eat this bread and drink this cup, you do *proclaim the Lord's death until He comes*" (1 Cor. 11:26, emphasis supplied). He comes to earth in the glory and majesty of His power, "mighty to save" (Isa. 63:1).

It is because of Christ and the gospel that a warning is given to and judgment pronounced on those who "add to, or take away, the words of the prophecies of this book" (Rev. 22:18, 19). Those who say, "Don't be concerned about Revelation; it has nothing for us today" are taking away. Christ's warning applies to them.

The blood of Christ is the emblem of His victory.

Revelation is "the word of God, and the testimony of Jesus Christ" (1:2). It is Christ's testimony for the church. It reveals things that Christ needed to tell His followers, for they could not have grasped them during His earthly ministry (see John 16:12).

Jesus, the Faithful and True Witness, closes Revelation by saying, "I Jesus have sent My angel to testify these things in the churches" (22:16). God's faithful people hear, keep, and teach the testimony that Christ gives in His Revelation (see 12:17).

REVELATION IS IMPORTANT! Notice the two prominent purposes of the book. Its first words are: "The revelation (the revealing, the unveiling) of Jesus Christ." Here is Jesus Christ, who in His life on earth won the victory over sin, Satan, and death. He is seated at the right hand of the Father. He shepherds

His church. He guides her in the closing work of the gospel (see Matt. 24:14).

Revelation Proclaims The Victory of Christ

Keep this fact in mind. Christ has won. The time when He will "make all things new" is certain. He offers His victory to "whoever will come" (Rev. 22:17).

Christ reveals things which would come to pass. He does not predict general history. He reveals those things which impact His gospel— His saving work on earth.

Revelation Unmasks Satan's Work to Destroy The Gospel And Church

This knowledge is necessary to not be deceived by Satan and keep faithful to Christ. Consider these observations by R.C.H. Lenski from his book *The Interpretation of St. John's Revelation*: "This book is in the highest sense Jesus Christ's book and the very language proclaims this great fact. John does the writing, but the very language is different from his own" (p. 16).

"We know indeed, from the Old Testament prophecies and from all the rest of the New Testament that Jesus is the Son of God and is now infinitely exalted on the throne of God in His human nature. Revelation unveils Him fully; it shows us the Tremendous Christ as He really is. The first vision, 1:9–20, presents Christ alone. It is overwhelming. John, who once reclined on Jesus' bosom, lay before Christ as one dead. This is the Christ with whom the universe and the church have to deal. Revelation unveils Him. If we could always carry this picture of Christ in our hearts, how much of our insipid discussion of Christ would utterly disappear! How much of our cheap treatment of His word, of our littleness of faith, our compromises with the world would vanish" (pp. 21, 22).

"The same is true with regard to Satan and his allies. The film that tends to becloud our eyes is removed. The whole satanic horror is here exposed. Our last illusions about Satan and his kingdom of darkness are dissipated" (p. 22). "The satanic power must work itself out, but its defeat and doom are absolutely certain. As the,

Living One, triumphed in His death, so He and His own ever triumph amid the raging of the dragon until the final judgment ends the conflict forever. This is the burden of Revelation" (p. 21).

Is it possible that in our rush to know about the "beast and its image" and "its mark", we rush passed Jesus? Christ does say, "I am showing you things that will come to pass", but if we do not first and foremost see our victorious Savior, we may focus on the terrors caused by the dragon, beast, and false prophet, and become afraid.

We are secure in Him who said, "These things I have spoken to you, that in Me you may have peace. In the world you have tribulation, but take courage; I have overcome the world" (John 16:33).

Why This Book?

For Christians living in the twenty-first century, Revelation is the Bible's most important book. The life and death of Christ is the greatest event of all time. God can perform no other act that could surpass it. Jesus Christ was and is the turning point of human history. By the birth, life, death, and resurrection of Jesus Christ, God *solved* the problem of sin, evil, and death. He has not yet *settled* the issue. The Bible reveals that that day is coming. For now, God gives to all of us life and breath that we might seek and find Him. He wants people to come to repentance and eternal life (see Acts 17:25, 27; 2 Pet. 3:9).

The book of Revelation, which the Apostle John scribed, is truth revealed by Jesus to guide His church in its earthly history, especially in the final days. "Surely the Lord God does nothing unless He reveals His secret counsel to His servants the prophets" (Amos 3:7).

Revelation gives a prophetic history of Christianity and reveals the victorious climax of the gospel of the Lord Jesus Christ.

This perspective on Revelation provides answers to the question, "How shall we understand this book?" Its first answer is, "We should focus on Revelation's two main themes."

It portrays our victorious Christ in His work to bring to completion all that was secured by His life on earth—"the restoration of all things..." (Acts 3:20, 21).

Revelation reveals Satan's work to destroy God's people and the gospel. Satan knows he is defeated and that his time is short, so, driven by great anger, he works against all people on earth (see Rev. 12:10, 12–17). How is it that Christianity, as presented to us through Jesus and taught by the apostles, has become what exists today? Is it all from God? No! Satan infiltrated Christianity to use it for his purposes of deception and destruction.

Daniel's prophecies predicted such work (see Dan. 7 and 8; also Acts 20:29, 30; 2 Thess. 2:3, 4). Paul's words to the church at Corinth fit well here: "In order that no advantage be taken of us by Satan; for we are not ignorant of his schemes" (2 Corinthians 2:11, NASB).

Revelation reveals much about Satan's war against Christ's end-time people, "the remnant...who keep the commandments of God and hold to the testimony of Jesus." Though he may appear "as an angel of light" (2 Cor. 11:2), he has one goal. The more people he can keep separated from God and on the path to destruction, the more hurt he inflicts on God.

Christ's declaration that all Scripture witnesses to Him (see John 5:39) and the following quotation have guided this study of Revelation.

> *"The Bible is its own expositor. Scripture is to be compared with scripture. The student should learn to view the Bible as a whole, and to see the relation of its parts. He should gain a knowledge of its grand central theme of God's original purpose for the world, of the rise of the great controversy, and of the work of redemption. He should understand the nature of the two principles that are contending for supremacy, and learn to trace their working through the records of history and prophecy to the great consummation. He should see how this controversy enters into every phase of human experience; how in every act of life he himself reveals one or the other of the two antagonistic motives; and how, whether he will or not, he is even now deciding upon which side of the controversy he will be found" (E.G. White, Education, p. 190).*

"Blessed is the person who reads, and those who hear the words of this prophecy, and keep the things that are written in it, for the time is near" (Rev. 1:3). Pray and ask God to enable you to receive the blessing of this book.

Why This Book?

A Helpful Note for Study

The books of Daniel and Revelation are companions. They have similar literary structures. Each of the prophetic sequences contained therein begins with the time of the writer and goes to the time when God delivers His people. Both books refer to a "forty-two month" or "1260 day" or "time, times, and half a time" prophetic period. Christ pointed out that Daniel's "abomination" was then still in the future (see Matt. 24:15). The little horn power of Daniel 7 and 8 does the same work as the beast of Revelation 13 does. They are identical. These prophecies of Daniel and Revelation enable us to determine where we are in God's great drama of salvation.

Daniel's great concern was for his people and Jerusalem. Babylon, with its armies, had destroyed Jerusalem. His heart broke over their situation. When would God's Messiah appear? When would God's promises for His people be realized?

The vision of Daniel 9 revealed that Jerusalem and the temple would be rebuilt. It gave the time when Messiah would come. It also stated that after Him would come more trouble. The city and the sanctuary would again be destroyed (in A.D. 70).

For Daniel and Christ's disciples, the Lord had things that they could not then bear. It was in mercy that some events were obscured from Daniel's understanding. God gave the promise that in the course of history, "the wicked will continue to be wicked. None of the wicked will understand, but the wise (God's people) will understand" (Dan. 12:10; see also Ps. 107:43). God's final words to Daniel were for him to keep trusting. He would enter into rest and rise again. He would be among those who "rise to everlasting life" and "shine like the stars for ever and ever" (Dan. 12:1–3, 13).

The following books give more details about the prophecies of Daniel and Revelation: *Daniel And Revelation* by Uriah Smith; *Unfolding The Revelation* by R.A. Anderson; *God Cares* by C. Mervyn Maxwell (Daniel and Revelation are covered in separate volumes); *The Great Controversy* by E.G. White.

Why Do We Believe?

Where Can We Anchor Our Lives? In What is Our Hope?

To say "The one true hope of the race is found in God" is not an adequate answer. Who is God? God must be identified. We anchor our lives and find our hope in the God of heaven and His Word, the Bible. Why do we do this? Why do we accept the words of Scripture as authoritative and not the words of Buddha, Confucius, Mohammed, or some other person who has claimed divine enlightenment? Why do we regard the Bible as different from other sacred literature? Why do we easily reject the teachings of gurus or someone who offers a new and improved "Christianity"?

The reason for our faith is found in the words "according to the scriptures" (1 Cor. 15:1–4). Jesus came out of Scripture. He appeared; His life was lived; His life was (susp)ended, and His life continues "according to the scriptures." That which Moses had written fourteen centuries prior to Christ's birth; that which was recorded in the Psalms a millennium beforehand; that which Isaiah had penned 700 years before the advent; the place of His birth foretold by the prophet Micah; all this and more were fulfilled in His life, death, and resurrection.

In the centuries before His birth, there was prophecy. God gave promises which were spoken and written by His prophets. Then Jesus was born, and by His life, He confirmed and fulfilled the prophecy and promises of God.

We Believe "According to The Scriptures"

Jesus Christ stands as more than a great teacher who appears in earth's scene and out of his own life teaches great, deep, spiritual truths. He presented Himself as the One foretold by the prophets. He came according to the plan of God. His life and teachings are not presented to us as a revolution—a breaking with the past. He did not present His teaching as something that had never been taught. He is the fulfillment of Scripture. As the fulfillment of Scripture, He is the connection that anchors us to the hope we have in God and His Word.

Because He comes out of Scripture from God, He becomes the interpreter of God and the Bible. "I will send My Son." He is "Emmanuel—God with us." "The Word was made flesh and lived among us" (Matt. 21:37; 1:23; John 1:14). This is the difference between Him and any other teacher that has or will come. We do not follow the ideas that are the product of human imagination and thinking, no matter how involved and appealing they might be.

Jesus presented Himself as not separate but united with the God of Scripture. He made constant reference to the Father.

He came from the Father (John 5:26, 37; 6:39, 57; 8:16, 18).

He did the works of the Father (John 5:26, 30; 6:38–40; 10:25).

He spoke the words of the Father (John 8:26, 28; 14:10, 24; 15:15; 17:18).

He claimed oneness with the Father (John 14:7–9; 17:21–26).

Jesus did not present Himself as separate from the Hebrew Old Testament.

"It is written" was His defense against temptation (Matt. 4:1–11).

He claimed the Scripture spoke about Him (John 5:39; Luke 24:25, 26, 44–47).

As the Son of Man, He did not present Himself as above Scripture. He was subject to it. To redeem Adam's failure, He must perfectly obey it (Matthew 5:17, 18).

As Son of God and Son of man, He was not divided against Himself.

As Messiah, the Son of Man, He was subject to Scripture. As God, He was above it, for it came from Him.

This is why His teaching was "with such authority." Both His life and teaching "magnified the law and made it great and glorious" (Isa. 42:21). His life and Word correct all the errors about God that result from human teaching. We have a strong,

Why Do We Believe?

logical reason for anchoring our hope in the authority of Scripture because it contains such a strong prophetic element that has been fulfilled in history.

The other basis for our faith is the work of the Spirit of God on our minds and hearts as we honestly consider His Word. Something happens within us. "Flesh and blood has not revealed it to you but My Father who is in heaven" (Matt. 16:17). We believe the Bible because it works; it makes sense out of life.

What it says will happen happens. This is seen in fulfilled prophecy. This is also true personally. The Spirit says, "Come." When we come, what He says will occur in our lives—forgiveness, peace, hope, joy, guidance, etc.—occurs.

The explanation the Bible presents for life as we experience it and see it in history is true. It tells us why life has become what it is. It tells us of God's grand purpose for individuals and the world. We see people coming to a new life. All He has promised and we hope for is made possible through the gift of God's Son. Jesus Christ is our Lord and Savior. We believe. Our faith rests in Him.

Revelation—Christ's Book of Victory

Some students at a seminary went to the gym one evening. They wanted to exercise and relax from their intense study. As they played basketball, the custodian of the gym sat at one side, reading his Bible. When the students finished, they went over to tell him so he could lock up. They saw he was reading from Revelation. "You are reading from Revelation?" they asked. "Yep," was his reply. They followed up with, "Do you understand that book?" Their thinking was, 'He is not a seminary student. How could he know?' "What does it say," they questioned. His answer was just four words: "God's going to win."

God's going to win. This is the assurance of Revelation. In spite of all the terrors to come that Revelation reveals, we can rest in confidence with God. God is going to win, for Christ has already gained the victory. The first thing one needs to know and keep in mind in a study of this book is that it proclaims Christ's victory.

> *God's going to win. This is the assurance of Revelation.*

In Revelation, all the claims that Christ made about Himself are seen as true. He has been enthroned with the Father. The unity of the Father, Christ, and the Holy Spirit is evident all through this book (see 1:1, 10; 2:7, 11, 17, etc.; 3:21; 21:22; 22:1). He is "The Lord of Glory." He prevailed in the battle with sin and Satan (see Ps. 24:7–10).

Armageddon's Glorious End

Jesus claimed that "all things that the Father has are mine" (John 16:15). Here we see the truth of this statement. Jesus sent it by His angel. The angels are His as much as they are the Father's. He is rightly called the Commander of the heavenly host.

The promise that God would "make him my firstborn, higher than the kings of the earth" (Psalm 89:27) has been realized. Jesus is the "Prince of the kings of the earth" and the "King of kings, and Lord of lords" (Rev. 1:5; 19:16).

John continues: "Unto Him that loved us and washed us from our sins by His own blood, and has made us a kingdom, and priests unto our God" (1:5, 6). Meditate upon this, and then with John proclaim what Christ's victory has provided for you, me, and "whosoever will come" (22:17). In chapter 5, the twenty-four elders near God's throne proclaim this same victory (see vs. 9, 10). This is followed by all the angels of heaven proclaiming the victory of Christ (see vs.11–14). The Lamb prevailed; glory, honor, and majesty belong to Him (see 1:7). John concludes his doxology of verses 5 and 6 with the "blessed hope."

"Behold He comes with clouds, and every eye shall see Him." Believers call it a "hope." To heaven, it is a reality, for Christ has gained the victory. The future that God planned and promised has been made sure. The Messiah has "brought in everlasting righteousness." The promises of prophecy have been sealed for fulfillment. The "most holy has been anointed" (Daniel 9:24). Our Great High Priest ministers for us in heaven. At the throne of God, Jesus, by His presence, makes a place for us (see John 14:1-3).

When Jesus cried from the cross "It is finished" (John 19:30), the victory was gained. There was a great earthquake. Graves broke open (see Matt. 27:51-53). Death was unsealed. When Jesus came out of His grave, "many who slept, came out of their graves and appeared to many." This fulfilled Isaiah 26:19: "Your dead men shall live, together with My dead body shall they arise. Awake and sing you that dwell in the dust...."

With the words "I am... the living One: I was dead and behold I am alive forevermore, and I have the keys of death and of Hades", Jesus proclaims His victory (Rev. 1:17, 18).

Revelation—Christ's Book of Victory

The serpent has received its death wound. The problem of sin and death has been solved. Though not yet settled, it will be settled in God's way, as promised by His prophets.

The many titles ascribed to Christ give evidence that by His life He was victorious over sin, and by His death, He became victorious over death (see Rev. 1:11, 17, 18; 2:1, 8, 12, 18; 3:1, 7, 14). Notice how He speaks to the churches. The church belongs to Him (see Rev. 2 and 3).

The descriptions of His glory and majesty reflect His prayer: "Father glorify Thou Me with the glory which I had with Thee before the world was" (John 17:5). Further ways in which Revelation proclaims the victory of Christ are seen as the book is studied. After we have in our minds and hearts Revelation's picture of our victorious Lord and Savior, we are then prepared for the rest of what Christ presents.

Satan has warred against God from the beginning. He worked to prevent God's promises of a Savior from ever unfolding. He was successful in keeping God's chosen nation from fulfilling its role as His servant. He worked personally against Christ.

Then he sought to destroy the young church. Evidence for this is found in the O.T., the Gospels, and the book of Acts. Not able to destroy it, he has worked to bring deceptions into Christianity and take it over to use it for his purposes.

More evidence of his war are the warnings against false teachings found in the N.T. letters. Paul specifically wrote of the coming of a "man of sin, who would sit in the temple of God" (2 Thess. 2:3, 4). In Revelation, we have Christ's words to the seven churches. His letters point out errors that were coming into the Christian faith. There were in each church those who heard what the Spirit said and kept true to Christ. There were many who embraced the errors and thus brought false worship into Christianity.

The preaching of the gospel of Christ changed the Roman Empire. By the time John wrote Revelation, this was evident (see Rev. 6:1–8). The first four seals portray Christianity as God's community. His kingdom was expanding, changing society and being changed by it. The apostolic church was portrayed as a "rider on a white horse [which] had gone forth conquering and to conquer."

The second, third, and fourth seals depicted persecution and a falling away from the purity of the gospel as Christianity became a dominant social force. Emperor Constantine, seeing the strength of Christianity, united it to his government. The resulting Christianity became so changed and adulterated that it persecuted and killed, rather than bring life.

The seven trumpets refer to warfare and other events that adversely affected Christianity. Revelation 12 briefly but graphically presents Satan's war against Christ and His church throughout the centuries. This earth-long warfare, first mentioned in Genesis 3:15, reaches its climax in Revelation. The final Christian apostasy (third woe) is depicted in 13:11–17.

Let us ever keep in mind the great victory that Revelation portrays. Christ is coming again for His people. There will be in heaven a great host of redeemed people. How many? More than can be numbered (see 7:9). Will you have faith and say, "In Christ, I can be one of them"? Go with Christ, and you will be on the winning side.

Making Sense Out of The Existence of Satan

If God is good, how can one make sense out of the existence of a devil? From where did Satan come? Why would a good God let him exist?

At the beginning of the Bible record, we find the serpent—Satan. When we turn to the New Testament and study the life of Jesus, we discover that before He did any teaching, preaching, or healing, He had a confrontation with the devil. As soon as He was baptized, Christ went into the wilderness and was tempted by Satan.

In the Bible's plot, it becomes very evident that more than just God and humans are involved. There are three parties involved. There is God. There is the human race. There is Satan.

From where did Satan come? How is he involved? Jesus says, "Come to Me. Learn of Me..." We can find the answer for the existence of Satan. When we learn from Christ in His Word, we can then make sense out of all that is going on in our world. We can find rest from all the meaningless and hopelessness that fills the world. In spite of the many conflicting ideas that swirl around us, we really can know the truth.

God tells us how to learn His truth, and it is certainly worth a try to do so. First, you ask God to enable you to understand His truth. "Knock...seek...ask" and "you will find" is His promise. The Holy Spirit is the "Spirit of truth." We cannot understand the Bible without the Holy Spirit giving us understanding. We must ask God for His Spirit. The Holy Spirit, who inspired the writers of the Bible, will enable us to understand it. What we experience is that the Holy Spirit first convicts us of our alienation from God. As we repent, He gives us a new life. He guides us into God's truth.

The second step in understanding God and His word is that we must be willing to know and do God's will. If we are only playing games with God, we find nothing. Jesus said, "If any man will do His will he shall know the doctrine..." (John 7:17). With Saul of Tarsus, we must ask, "Lord, what will you have me to do?" and be willing to do it. Too many people spend their lives making excuses to avoid God. The Scripture says that a "double-minded person will not receive any wisdom from the Lord." "You will seek Me and find Me, when you search for Me with all your heart" (James 1:5–8; Jer. 29:13).

Isaiah 28:9–13 gives us the next step. It asks the question, "To whom will God teach knowledge?" The answer is to those "weaned from milk." That means to one who is established in Christ and is growing spiritually. Then it says, "line upon line, here a little, there a little." This means we are to compare one Scripture with another. As God gave His Scriptures over the centuries, His truth became brighter and brighter, clearer and clearer. One prophet would speak, then another. By comparing and uniting the points of truth from the various writers, a correct understanding of God's word is developed. "In the mouth of two or three witnesses let a thing be established," is another guiding principle in learning truth.

Jesus followed this method in teaching His disciples, especially following His resurrection. He said the prophets had spoken about the sufferings of the Messiah (see Luke 24:25–27; 44, 45). He started with Moses, and then went to all the other prophets to establish them in the truth that He was the promised Messiah. Jesus confirmed the "here a little, there a little" motif, and the disciples saw that His whole life—ministry, suffering, death, and resurrection—all fit into what the prophets had spoken centuries previously. Their faith in Him was established by Bible study.

We can do the same and get the answers regarding who Satan is and from where he came. The word "Satan" means "adversary" and "accuser." "Satan" is not a Greek word, though it appears more in the New Testament than in the Old. It is a Hebrew word. The New Testament writers, using the Greek alphabet, simply spelled out the Hebrew word.

Matthew, Mark, and Luke tell us that after Jesus was baptized, the Spirit led Him into the wilderness, where He was tempted by the devil. The word for "devil" is *diabolos*. It means "slanderer"—one who falsely and maliciously accuses another of wrongdoing. We know about such slander from our political campaigns. All kinds of accusations are made about an opponent. That is what Satan did to God.

Jesus referred to Satan as "the prince of devils" (Matt. 12:24). As the prince of devils, Satan has many helpers. Jesus also referred to "the devil and his angels" (Matt. 25:41). Satan is not alone in his work.

In John 8:44, Jesus said that Satan is the father of lusts, murder, and lies. Satan tries to make people believe that all these evil things come from God. They don't come from God. They come from Satan. He is the deceiver of the whole earth.

Jesus also called Satan "the prince of this world." Three times he is referred to by this title (see John 12:31; 14:30; 16:11). How can Satan be the "prince of this world"? He gained the dominion that had been given to Adam and Eve. When he tempted Christ, Satan "showed Him all the kingdoms of the world in a moment of time" and said that it had been delivered to him. Jesus did not dispute Satan's claim (see Luke 4:5, 6). Satan had made the same claim in the story of Job. There he appeared before God as the one who had authority on earth. Adam could not be there. He was dead. Jesus came to break the rule of Satan and bring salvation to earth's inhabitants.

From Where Did Satan and His Angels Come?

The Apostle Peter spoke of "the angels that sinned and were cast down" (2 Peter 2:4). Jude tells us that there were angels who did not remain in their proper position but left it (see v. 6). They will be punished in the judgment of the great day. When Jesus spoke about Satan in John 8:44, He said the devil "abode not in the truth." He was once in God's truth, but he left it. Now he has nothing to do with truth. He works through deception.

The Bible tells us there are fallen angels. God did not make them fallen. They became fallen. Jesus said, "I beheld Satan as lightning fall from heaven" (Luke 10:18).

Revelation 12:3–9 portrays Satan's war against God and His people. It tells us that the war began in heaven (see v. 7). Michael and His angels fought against the dragon and his angels, and "the great dragon, that old serpent called the devil and Satan who deceives the whole world was cast out into the earth, and his angels were cast out with him." Verse 4 says that one-third of the angels followed Satan.

Taking what Jesus, Peter, John, and Jude said and putting it all together, we begin to get the picture. Satan and his angels were not created evil angels by God. They were good. They were in heaven, and there they rebelled. But why? How could it happen?

The prophets Isaiah and Ezekiel add more to our understanding. Using the " King of Tyrus" figure, Ezekiel 28:11–19 gives us more information. He was "full of wisdom and perfect in beauty" (v. 12). He had been in Eden, the garden of God, and was created with musical ability. Verse 14 calls him "the anointed cherub that covers." That means he stood next to the throne of God. "You were perfect in your ways from the day you were created, until iniquity was found in you" (vs. 15). He was created perfect, but he sinned. Verse 17 states what happened: "Your heart was lifted up because of your beauty. You corrupted your wisdom by reason of your brightness."

This created being in heaven had received great and wonderful gifts from his Creator. He joyfully served his Maker. He received honor and praise. After a while, he focused on himself. He gloried in his gifts, abilities, and position. His thinking became corrupted when he focused on himself. He did not want to keep God at the center of his life. He wanted all to say how great he was.

Isaiah tells us how far he went in his proud thinking (Isaiah 14:12–14). "How you are fallen from heaven, O Lucifer—shining one:" Here we find his name was Lucifer. Lucifer said, "I will exalt my throne above the stars of God...I will ascend above the heights of the clouds. I will be like the most high." He coveted the place of God. First, he said these things in his heart. He only thought them. Then he began to raise questions, insinuations, and accusations in the minds of the other angels, raising doubts about how good God was. He won angels to his side. Finally, there was war in heaven, and he was cast out.

Lucifer said, "I will be like the Most High." What is wrong with that? Why couldn't Lucifer be God? Because he could not create. He could not give life. This is the gulf between Creator and creature. To be God, one must be able to create a world, life on it, and keep it going. Though it was impossible for Satan to be God, he coveted the position and honor that goes to the Creator. He wanted to be treated as number one.

After Rebelling, Why Were Satan and His Angels Not Destroyed?

Suppose God worked that way. As soon as one differed with Him, he was destroyed. Just raise one question about God, and you've had it. What kind of God would He be?

We hear of governments that work that way. They have "thought police." People disappear. They are never seen again, or they are found dead, just for saying something against the government. What kind of governments are those that do such things? If God worked that way, fear, not love, would be the rule. Angels, and we too, would say, "Lucifer must have been right. God is not fair. He is not kind. He is a brutal despot." God's government is not based on force and fear.

God is love. His government is based on His love. God did something much more difficult than destroying. He suffered because of the rebellion of Satan and his angels. He suffered because of sin in heaven. He suffered even more when Adam and Eve disobeyed Him. God's love provided a way to save and restore us. The truth is, "God was in Christ reconciling the world unto Himself" (2 Corinthians 5:19).

At the cross, the power of love in Jesus stands out in sharp contrast to the lust for power in Satan. "God so loved the world that He gave His only Son." Self-sacrificing love is God's character and rule. Getting, taking, and self-aggrandizement are the characteristics of the rule of Satan and our world.

By the life and death of Jesus, Satan has been forever defeated. In Jesus, God is revealed. He is the God of love, grace, and truth. His death pays the penalty for our sin. He forgives and restores us.

God did not immediately destroy Satan and his angels. God let sin develop. He is letting the harvest of sin ripen so that all created beings in heaven and on earth will see the results of disobedience. Disobeying God does not bring good. Sin brings only suffering and death.

Satan knows he is defeated. He knows he has only a short time. He does not give up. He still devours and destroys (see Rev. 12:12; 1 Pet. 5:8). The way he tries to hurt God is to get people to be lost with him. His delight is to hurt and destroy.

One day soon, Satan will be gone. At the end of the world, "the devil that deceived them was cast into the lake of fire and brimstone" (Rev. 20:10). Satan is not in charge of the fire. Jesus said the fire "was prepared for the devil and his angels" (Matt. 25:41). Don't be in Satan's harvest.

The issue is not Satan and his power. The issue is Jesus. He gained the victory over sin, Satan, and death. He solved the problem of sin. Sin is not yet settled, but it will be in the judgment. What are you doing with the power of His gospel as it touches your life? Are you staying with Satan and rejecting Jesus? We are in this great, cosmic plot. We are confronted by Jesus on the cross. He calls out, "I died for you. I have forgiveness for you. Come! Come! Receive My life."

The Christ of Revelation

Do You Know the Christ of Revelation? What Does the Book of Revelation Add to What We Know About Christ?

The four Gospels present to us the man Christ Jesus. Born of a woman, we see Him as One with us. He grew up in Nazareth. He became a teacher and healer. He needed food. He got tired and needed sleep. He felt joy and sorrow. He suffered. He died. However, He was more than another human. He was "Emmanuel"—God with us.

The rest of the New Testament keeps expanding this picture of who He is. The book of Hebrews portrays Him in His unique, Melchizedekian priesthood.

It is in the book of Revelation that He is presented in all His victorious majesty. The book begins: "The revelation of Jesus Christ which God gave to Him, to show His bond-servants the things that must shortly take place..." Curiosity causes us to focus on the second part of this sentence—"the things that are going to happen." That is what we want to know. For what events shall we look? Many are given. They are presented in symbolic language—seven lamp stands, seven seals, trumpets, beasts, plagues, a mysterious number 666, etc. We are fascinated by these things.

Do we want to know what is coming? Can we know? Yes, the Lord does give us understanding. How? By studying these things with a prayerful, open, and willing mind. Compare Scripture with Scripture, letting the Bible interpret itself (see Hebrews 5:12–6:1).

We have gained much understanding about "the things that must shortly take place." However, what about the first part of the first sentence of this book?

Do You Know the Christ of Revelation?

In the face of all the evil presented in this book, we can rest secure in Christ and His Word. Christ gained the victory over sin, death, and any and every antagonistic power in the universe (see Eph. 6:12; Col. 2:15). Do you go forward knowing all power in heaven and earth is His? Do you, by faith, make His victory your victory?

Revelation 1 introduces Jesus Christ. Verse 5 begins to reveal His victory. He is the "First of earth's kings." This fulfills Psalm 89:27. Also, "He loved us and washed us from our sins in His own blood."

Zechariah 13:1 prophesied of a fountain for cleansing that would be opened. It is done. "The fountain is opened," for He gained the victory!

Isaiah 53:4–11 promised God's Suffering Servant who would bear our sins, heal us, and justify us. It is done. He bore our sins. He gained the victory. Four more times in Revelation, we are reminded that it was by His death and blood that He gained the victory for us (see 5:9; 7:14; 12:11; 19:13).

Jesus often said, "The kingdom of heaven is like..." "He has made us [His followers] to be a kingdom, priests to God" (1:6). Christians are not called a "nation." The word for nation is *ethnos*—meaning a racial, ethnic group. Christ's followers come from every nation and language. They would not be a nation as was Israel or other nations. Christ takes people from every race and translates them into His kingdom (see Col. 1:13). Peter refers to Christians as a "holy nation" (1 Peter 2:9, 10). The "ethnicity" that makes Christians a nation is not race, but "holiness". Worldly citizenship is subjected to the new citizenship in Christ's kingdom. Christians have pledged themselves to be completely the Lord's—to live His way. That is what it means to be a "holy nation". Revelation 1:6 and 1 Peter 2:9 essentially say that Christ has made us a kingdom of priests. We are separated to live our lives as a witness for God (see Rom. 12:1). "Whatever your hand finds to do, do it heartily as unto the Lord not to men" (Col 3:23).

The calling that was given to Israel has passed to His church (see Ex.19:5, 6; Deut. 7:6; 1 Pet. 2:10). This is our calling. We are His witness. His victory gives to us the privilege to come personally before God. We no longer need an earthly mediator upon whom we must depend.

His victory is the guarantee that He is coming again, and "every eye will see Him" (Rev. 1:7). In verses 11–16, we see Christ in His eternity and deity, "glorified with the glory He had with the Father before the world was." In "the Son of Man", humanity is carried to the throne of God. "We are adopted in the Beloved."

In verses 17–20, we find that Christ is the "Living One." He was dead but is now alive forever. He holds the keys of death and the grave. His first priority is His church, for His church is His light in the world, the agency through which God will accomplish His purpose. Christ is in the midst of His church, engaged in untiring ministry. He is connected to her as is the head to the body. "He that keeps His people shall neither slumber or sleep" (Ps. 121:3, 4).

The message that God sends to us in this book is not separate from, or contrary to, the gospel. It assures us that the life, death, and resurrection of Jesus Christ has made certain "the restoration of all things". Notice the words "blood" and "Lamb" in the following verses: 1:5; 5:9; 7:14; 12:11.

This brings us to the Lamb of Revelation. Abraham, speaking to Isaac on Mt. Moriah, where God had directed him to offer Isaac, said, "God will provide for Himself the lamb for the burnt offering, my son..." (Genesis 22:8). Abraham named that place "The Lord will provide" (Genesis 22:14).

Isaiah 53 tells of the Suffering Servant who will be led as a lamb to the slaughter (after Pentecost, Christ's disciples preached that this was fulfilled by Jesus (see Acts 8:32–35). God's appointed forerunner of His Messiah, John the Baptist, introduced Jesus as "the Lamb of God who bears away the sins of the world" (John 1:29, 36). Christ is also referred to as the Lamb in 1 Peter 1:19. In the book of Revelation, there are twenty-eight references to Christ as "The Lamb" (the first is Rev. 5:6).

Chapter 5 provides further insight regarding the Christ of Revelation. There is a sealed book (eventually it is discovered that the book contains God's eternal purpose for our earth. Adam and Eve's sin canceled that purpose and set the world on the road to decay and death). Who could solve the dilemma? No one could be found. It appeared hopeless John greatly wept.

Then, good news is announced: "The Lion of Judah, The Root of David, has prevailed." He has overcome all the inabilities of angels, humans, and all creation. "The Lion of Judah, the Root of David." Those words suggest a majestic, mighty warrior, so John looks to see, and what does he see? David with Goliath's head? No. There, in the center of the throne, he sees a Lamb, standing as if slain.

> *Every decision heaven makes is made regarding the Lamb who was slain and is now on the throne with the Father.*

The Lamb advances and takes the book, and when He did, a mighty chorus peels out—music such as earth has never heard, more majestic than Handel's Hallelujah Chorus. The twenty-four elders prostrate themselves before the Lamb in worship and praise. Thousands of angels join them in giving honor and praise to the Lamb. John's tears are turned into joy (and so are mine).

Do you see the Lamb of Revelation? Are your tears and sorrow over your life turned into joyfulness, and are you led in wonder to worship Him?

Behold what has happened to the Lamb of Isaiah 53—the despised, suffering Lamb; the One that people condemned, enjoying His suffering because they said God was punishing Him. The despised Lamb has become the victorious, enthroned, worship-worthy Christ. Do you see the Lamb—the Christ of Revelation? All power is His!

Our human race is not done with Him. All of us will face Him one final time (see 6:14–17). Every decision heaven makes is made regarding the Lamb who was slain and is now on the throne with the Father.

The Christ of Revelation

Starting in Revelation 6, The Lamb broke the seals one by one. The events there portrayed occurred. Christianity as a society was changed. The "little horn" power of Daniel 7 and 8 manifested itself, and the glorious gospel was changed to a ministry of death.

Christ has not lost control. Judgment is passed "in favor of the saints." Humanity trembles before the Lamb who at last must reward them with wrath (see 6:16; 14:10).

"Who is able to stand" (6:17)? Who can stand before God and the Lamb? Revelation 7 shows us those who can stand. It is those who have washed their robes and made them white in the blood of the Lamb. God's sealing work has enabled them to stand. God has His people. At last, they will be with Him.

Revelation 7:9–17 tells us it is the Lamb that has made this possible. This is further pictured in chapter 14. Have you heard the music? Do you have the Lamb's victory song singing in your heart? They sing the victory song, the song of Moses and the Lamb (see Rev. 15:3). How is it that they were able to be "overcomers"? It is "because of the blood of the Lamb, and because of the word of their testimony" (Rev. 12:11, NASB).

Revelation 13:8 speaks of the Lamb's book of life and those whose names are written there. The appeal is made. You have ears. Are you hearing—responding to this appeal? To enter God's holy city, one's name must be in the Lamb's book of life (21:27). All the way through Revelation, it is the Lamb, the Lamb, the Lamb! It was the death of the sinless Son of God that brought victory.

Satan still relentlessly wages "war with the Lamb, but the Lamb overcomes them" (Rev. 17:14). All through history, Satan has carried on his strategy against Christ and His church. He has used people, organizations, religions, and nations to do this. He has worked to destroy Christ's gospel. His final war is against the remnant who are true to the Lamb.

Revelation 13 sets the stage for the final conflict. What a conflict! What a contrast we see! Satan has a counterfeit, triune committee: himself (the dragon), the seven-headed, ten-horned monster, and the lamb–like false prophet. To human eyes and knowledge, it appears to be no contest.

SURPRISE! THE LAMB HAS WON! THE LAMB HAS WON!

Armageddon's Glorious End

This is the Christ of Revelation. Do you know Him? Behold the Lamb! Do not keep your focus on the beast and all he does. We have the rest of the story. Behold the victorious Lamb! (see Rev. 19:1–9). He is at the throne of God for us. He wants us to join Him there. God and the Lamb are the Temple and the Light of the New Jerusalem (see 21:22, 23). Also, the throne of God and the Lamb is there (see 22:3). Make it your life goal to be there.

Revelation's Unity and Order of Events

John was told to "write in a book" what he was shown and send it to the seven churches. It is one book not seven books. The events given in Revelation begin with the time of John and close with all things made new. There is a unity in its structure.

One piece of evidence for the unity of Revelation is how it begins and closes with identical thoughts. The entire book is a testimony of Christ for the church (see 1:4 and 22:16). Revelation begins with a blessing and ends with the same blessing (see 1:3 and 22:7).

Christ promised, "I will come again" (John 14:3). This promised event is presented in Revelation 1:7 and 22:7, 12, and 20.

This unity does not mean that Revelation is a one-line chronology of events. The five separate descriptions of the return of Christ make this clear. The book is composed of several groups of visions that run parallel to each other. They reinforce and expand Christ's prophetic picture of the age–long conflict between Christ and Satan. Each group pictures events which culminate in the return of Christ in power and glory. "Behold I come quickly" is Christ's word to Philadelphia, the sixth of the seven churches (see 3:11). The sixth seal presents the terror of the world at His appearing (see 6:14–17).

Following the vision of the seals comes the vision of the seven trumpets (see 8:6–11:19). After the sixth trumpet comes the mighty, heavenly message: "time no more shall be" (10:6,7). Prophecy is being fulfilled. The day is near, but "you must prophesy again" (10:11).

Armageddon's Glorious End

The sounding of the seventh trumpet brings another picture of "the end" (see 11:15–19). In Revelation 12–14, one will find the transition from the historical events which impacted Christianity to end–time events. Chapter 12 depicts Satan and his age–long war against God. It began in heaven, but Satan was cast out. Next, he waged war against the "man–child." Again, he failed. Then he attacked the "woman"—the church—and finally, he wars against the "remnant of her seed." Chapter 13 depicts Satan's war through the beast powers to destroy the woman (God's people and truth) and climaxes with his war against the "remnant". Revelation 14:1–12 depicts God's faithful people and the messages that kept them faithful. The three messages (vs. 6–12) prepare the harvest of the earth [14:13–20; "The harvest is the end of the world" (Matt. 13:39)]. This is the third time the end is pictured. Following the seventh plague, the end of this world is again presented (see 16:17–21).

The final portrayal of Christ's coming is in Revelation 19:11–21. There we see Jesus Christ in glorious majesty as "King of kings and Lord of lords." The beast and the false prophet are thrown into the lake of fire, and all who followed them are killed.

These five pictures of Christ's return make it clear that the prophecies do not present a one–line chronology. They give the understanding which the church needs to keep faithful to God and give the message of Christ to all the world.

Dr. William H. Shea, in his book *Daniel*, offers further understanding of this fact based on what's found in Daniel 7, 8, and 9:

"In terms of (the chronology of) the events to which these prophecies refer, chapter 9 comes first because it focuses especially on the Messiah. The contents of chapter 8, go well beyond that point into the Christian Era. But it is chapter 7 which carries the prophecy on to the final kingdom of God and pictures the saints of the Most High as entering and possessing it.

"There is a reason for following this thought order... In modern western–European thought, we reason from cause to effect. We collect all the data and then synthesize it into a hypothesis. Finally we refine that hypothesis to a theory. This is the procedure of the

Revelation's Unity and Order of Events

modern scientific method. "But the ancients were not moderns... They worked out things their own way. While they were quite capable of working through things in a chronological order as we do, they also utilized an approach that involved reasoning from effect back to cause. The prophets could depict a scene that led the listeners to inquire. Why did this happen?' This question led them back to the cause. An inspired prophet could say, 'This land will be destroyed and left desolate,' leading back to the natural question, Why will this land be destroyed?' The answer to that question commonly lay in the fact that the people to whom the prophet was sent were a wicked and rebellious people, who had broken their covenant with God" (p. 14).

This way of presenting information is common in Scripture. The prophet speaks the Lord's decision. After the decision is given, then is presented the causes for the decision. Once we are aware of this way of providing information, it can be observed in some instances in Scripture. In Genesis 6:3–13, God said He would give man 120 years. Then He gives the reason for His decision.

In Revelation, the various scenes in each group of visions are not necessarily in strict chronological order. They are complementary. They enlarge the picture. This knowledge helps one understand how the visions fit together. The prophecies of Revelation, combined with those of Daniel, give us a panorama of the age–long war in which the Lamb of God and His church stand victorious.

Symbols in the Visions of Revelation

The Lord used many symbols in giving the message of this book to His church. The dictionary definition of "symbol" is "something that stands for, represents another thing."

Revelation 1:12–16 presents us with seven golden lampstands, seven stars, and a majestic Son of Man—Jesus Christ—with tokens of His deity. His face shone like the sun with a sword coming out of His mouth. The meaning of the lampstands and stars is given in verse 20. The other symbols are identified by their use elsewhere in the Bible.

The following passages enable us to understand the symbol of the sword of His mouth:

"The sword of the Spirit is the word of God" (Eph. 6:17).

"He brought us forth by the word of truth" (James 1:18).

"The word of God is living... sharper than any two–edged sword" (Heb. 4:12).

"All Scripture is inspired by God, and is profitable for ... righteousness" (2 Tim. 3:16).

"The word that I spoke will judge him at the last day" (John 12:48).

> *Bible history and Christian history reveal that it is through accepting and obeying the Word of God that the church remains faithful to God and able to accomplish its mission.*

Bible history and Christian history reveal that it is through accepting and obeying the Word of God that the church remains faithful to God and able to accomplish its mission.

Christ wanted to keep the Pergamos Church true to Him (see Rev. 2:16). In His counsel to them, He said that if they did not repent and reject the errors they were embracing, He would fight against them with the sword of His mouth. His Word, impressed by the power of the Holy Spirit, pierced their conscience; they knew what their choice should be. He urged them "to hear what the Spirit was saying to them." The teaching of the Word of God, in opposition to human tradition, became the issue in the Protestant Reformation and continues.

Other symbols in the book of Revelation and other apocalyptic prophecies of the Bible are to be understood in the same way. Thus, the Bible becomes its own interpreter.

The Number 7 in the Book of Revelation

Symbolism is prominent in the book of Revelation. Most of the symbols can be understood by their use in other books of the Bible. Numbers, besides having their numerical value, can also have a symbolic significance. Most prominent in Revelation is the number seven. It appears forty-nine times. What is its symbolic meaning?

"There is clear evidence in the cuneiform texts, which are our earliest authorities, that the Babylonians regarded 7 as the number of totality, of completeness. The Sumerians, from whom the Babylonians seem to have borrowed the idea, equated 7 and "all." The seven–storied towers of Babylonia represented the universe. 7 was the expression of the highest power, the greatest conceivable fullness of force, and therefore was early pressed into the service of religion. It is found in reference to ritual in the age of Gudea, that is perhaps about the middle of the 3d millennium B.C. "Seven gods," at the end of an enumeration meant, "all the gods.". As this sacred or symbolic use of 7 was not peculiar to the Babylonians and their teachers and neighbors, but was more or less known also in India and China, in classical lands, and among the Celts and Germans" (William Taylor Smith, *International Standard Bible Encyclopedia*, vol. iv, p. 2159).

This idea of completeness is derived from God's activity. "Thus the heavens and the earth were completed, and all their hosts. And on the seventh day God completed His work which He had done; and He rested on the seventh day from all the work which He had done" (Gen. 2:1, 2). The idea of seven symbolizing "completeness" is evident in this and other references throughout Scripture (see Gen. 4:14, 15; Matt. 12:45; 18:21, 22; etc.).

In Revelation, the seven named churches are used to represent the complete Christian age. The seven spirits of God equal the completeness of the Holy Spirit at work in the world. The many sevens remind us that Christ is completing His work of salvation on the earth.

In seeking to understand from where the idea of seven and rest originated, Augustus Strong, in *Systematic Theology* (A.D. 1907) gives various ideas and quotes the following:

"But now the discovery of a calendar tablet in Mesopotamia shows us the week of seven days and the Sabbath in full sway in ancient Babylon long before the days of Moses. In this tablet the seventh, the fourteenth, the twenty–first, and the twenty–eighth, are called Sabbaths, the very word used by Moses, and following it are the words: 'A day of rest.' The restrictions are as rigid in this tablet as those in the law of Moses. This institution must have gone back to the Accadian period, before the days of Abraham. In one of the recent discoveries this day is called, 'the day of rest for the heart,' but of the gods, on account of the propitiation offered that day, their heart is at rest. See Jastrow, in Am. Jour. Theo. April 1898" (p. 408).

"A rest for the gods" is reflective of Genesis 2:2, but the idea that the "rest for the gods" is due to some propitiation (something humans have done for the gods) is a corruption of God's rest on the seventh day and gift of the Sabbath rest to humanity. The understanding of the number seven symbolizing completeness arose out of God's activity in the creation of the world and is seen in His use of the number in speaking to Cain (see Gen. 4:15).

The Seven Churches

It is helpful to review the setting for the giving of Revelation. All the apostles except John were dead. Jerusalem and the temple had been destroyed by Titus and his army (A.D. 70). Jesus had foretold this destruction: "not one stone shall be left upon another" (Matt. 24:3).

The disciples had asked, "When shall these things be. What will be the sign of Your coming and the end of the world?" To the disciples, the destruction of the temple and the return of Christ would occur close together. In giving the signs of "these things", Jesus answered their question the same way they had asked it. He did not separate which signs applied to which event. This is because, in the destruction of Jerusalem, there are lessons for those living in the end–time (see Matt. 24:4–51). The early believers longed for and anticipated the return of Christ (see 1 Cor. 1:7). They had questions: "Why the delay? Where is Christ? What is He doing?"

In His Revelation, Christ gave light and hope for those early Christians and all believers. Daily we hear reports of all that humans are doing in our world. There is so much tragedy; so much evil. We too wonder, 'When will Christ return and end all evil?' The assurance of Revelation is that in spite of all these events, the purpose for which Jesus lived and died is moving to its goal (see Acts 3:20, 21). "Behold I come quickly."

Today, Christianity exists in many forms in the world. How are we to understand Christianity as it has developed and now exists in the world? The various and conflicting forms of Christianity that exist cannot all be the work of God. How did Christianity change from the way Christ lived it and the New Testament teaches it to the current manifestation—Roman Catholicism, Eastern Orthodoxy, patriarchs and popes, national churches, and the many churches that have come into existence since the Protestant Reformation?

The Seven Churches and Seals are a Prophecy of Christianity

The seven churches of Revelation 2 and 3 reveal how Christianity was changed. Addressed to the seven named churches, the messages have meaning for all Christians, for each message concludes with the words, "he that has ears to hear let him hear what the Spirit says to the churches." God had more than those seven congregations in mind in giving Revelation. The seven churches are a prophecy of Christianity from the time of the apostles to the second coming of Christ. The prophetic purpose of the messages to the seven churches and the unlatching of the seven seals is to give us heaven's view of the development of Christianity. The Bible, especially the prophecies of Daniel and Revelation, contains answers to why Christianity has become such a babel of beliefs.

Jesus appeared to John as "The Son of Man", yet exercising the attributes and functions of His deity (see Rev. 1:10–20). Christ had promised His disciples: "I will never leave you nor forsake you" and "all authority has been given me in heaven and on earth" (Matt. 28:18, 20; Heb. 13:5, NKJV). He revealed Himself, standing in the midst of the seven churches and holding their messengers in His hand. The victorious Christ loves and guides His church.

The War Against Christ's Church and His Gospel

During His earthly ministry, Jesus warned His followers that "false teachers, and false prophets" would arise. They are "wolves in sheep's clothing", even working miracles. Many would be deceived by them (Matthew 7:15, 20–24; 24:5, 11, 24). His enemy would not only cause persecution but would scatter tares among the good seed (see Matt 13:25, 26).

The devil's deception had begun when he, through the serpent, lied to Eve. It continued through human history. Satan, as an angel of light, came to Christ in the wilderness, seeking to deceive Him. Satan tempted Jesus to engage in false practices: "make these stones bread"; "throw yourself down and prove you are the son of God."

He who was from eternity was born into this world as a human. To become our Savior, He must live His life as a human, not as God. The only way for Him to break the dominion which the "the prince of this world" had over humans was to resist and overcome him. To enter into a bargain with him and worship him would mean failure.

Christ also told His followers that He was not forsaking them. His going was for their benefit. With Pentecost, they experienced that it was so. He, at the throne of God, was the cause of why the Holy Spirit came and worked with such power (see Acts 2:33).

As we read Revelation, we see that Christ's first concern is His church—His people. Before He spoke of disasters—trumpets, dragon, beasts, mark, and plagues—the religious, political, and national events that would war against His truth—He pictured for us His care for His people.

He walks in the midst of His churches. He holds the ministers of the churches in His right hand. His Word (the sword of His mouth) is their strength (see Rev. 1:12, 16, 20). "He loved us and released us from our sins by His own blood. He has made us His kingdom, priests to God and His Father" (Rev. l:5, 6). This is the picture to carry in our minds, for if Christ does not have a faithful people, then He has nothing—no witness in the world.

Christ begins by giving His testimonies for the seven churches (Rev. 2 and 3). To each of the seven, He gives commendation for their faithfulness and right doing. He then warns them by revealing more about Satan's war against His gospel and church. Each message closes with a special promise for everyone who "overcomes".

The way He identifies Himself to each church reminds us that He is all sufficient. No matter how the present situation challenges our faith, He enables us to be faithful. His seven promises remind us of His victory, and that our security is in Him.

To each church, the Spirit pleads: whoever has ears, hear and obey what the Spirit is saying. In each church age, there were those who heard and kept faithful. There were also many who did not hear. They followed the deceptions coming into Christianity. The first four of the seven seals more specifically reveal what happened to Christianity.

Jesus is depicted as being in the midst of the seven named churches. There were more than seven churches in Asia Minor. Colossae, Militus, Asos, and Troas, which are all mentioned in the book of Acts, were near these seven. Christ's care for them is no less. Of the seven named churches, just two—Ephesus and Laodicea—are mentioned elsewhere in the New Testament. For the other five churches, this is the only reference to them in the Bible.

"The cities where the seven churches existed lay along the imperial post road. This Roman highway was built about 133 B.C. It passed through Ephesus, Smyrna, Pergamos, Thyatira, Sardis, Philadelphia, and Laodicea, where it joined another post highway."

The War Against Christ's Church and His Gospel

"Ephesus was a leading commercial city. By imperial edict, it was made the gateway to the province of Asia and became the starting place of the land trade route" (R.A. Anderson, *Unfolding The Revelation*, pp. 6, 16).

The imperial post road, which the Emperor used to send messages to his subjects, was symbolically used by the Lord to give His message to His kingdom.

The entire book of Revelation is addressed "to the seven churches which are in Asia" (Rev. 1:4,11; 22:16). It was written in one book, not seven different books. The messages are for more than the named church. They are universal, for repeated in each message are the words, "He that has ears to hear, let him hear what the Spirit says to the churches."

The book of Revelation presents events from apostolic times to the return of Christ and the establishment of God's New Jerusalem. Its messages involve the whole world.

The number seven, both in the Bible and ancient history, symbolized completeness. The messages did apply to the situation in the seven local churches, but they also represent Christianity during different periods of Christian history.

"The names of the seven churches are symbolic of the church in different periods of the Christian era…The number seven indicates completeness, and is symbolic of the fact that the messages extend to the end of time…The symbols used reveal the condition of the church at different periods in the history of the world" (E.G. White, *The Acts of The Apostles*, p. 585).

The descriptions given are accurate to historical events of the named cities. The events are used as instructive lessons for all Christians. As prophecies of Christianity, the messages to the seven churches are vital to the understanding of the rest of the book [the dragon's war against the woman and her offspring (Rev. 12:13–17) is already evident in the situations against which Christ warns in these messages; recommended reading: RA. Anderson, *Unfolding The Revelation*, chapters 3, 4, and 5; C. Mervyn Maxwell, *God Cares*, vol. 2—Revelation].

The name "Ephesus" (Rev. 2:1–7) means "desirable". Its desirable location made it the gateway to Asia. Ephesus had apostles to guide it. The church was faithful to the word of Christ. They rejected evil people. They tested those who claimed to be apostles but were not. They would not accept the behavior of the Nicolaitans as acceptable for Christ's followers. This tells us that false teachers and teachings were attempting to infiltrate Christianity. Jesus' rebuke for Ephesus was: "You have left your first love." Evidently, their concern for correct teaching had eclipsed compassion for people. Gospel zeal was gone. If we see our task as exposing error, it is easy to look at people suspiciously. We forget that we are not called to be detectives, but witnesses for Jesus Christ. Yes, we are to "try the spirits, for many false spirits are in the world." However, the first mission of the church is to "seek and save the lost." If love for the people around us is lost, the church fails.

The name "Smyrna" (Rev. 2:8–11) means "sweet smelling" and is synonymous with myrrh. No rebuke is given to Smyrna. Tribulation and poverty are methods Satan uses to cause people to give up faith in Christ and do what is popular. The reference to "those who say they are Jews but are not, but are a synagogue of Satan" must refer to those who claim to be the God's people but are not true followers of Christ. They introduced false teachings (see Rom. 2:28, 29; 1 Cor. 12:13; Gal. 3:26–29; Matt. 7:21–23).

The name "Pergamos" (Rev. 2:12–17) means "height, elevation". The city was built on an elevation of 1,000 feet. This church is said to be located "where Satan's throne is." Lucifer aspired to ascend to the heights of God. Some years after Babylon was overthrown, the priests of Babylon led a revolt against the Persians. They were defeated and fled and fixed their central college at Pergamos. They took the palladium of Babylon, the cubic stone, with them (R.A. Anderson cites this record in his book. Later, when the king of Pergamos bequeathed his dominion to the emperor, the Babylonian system was transferred to Rome).

In Pergamos, Christ's faithful witness, Antipas, had been killed. "Balaam" indicates the idea that Christians should compromise with the world and thus gain worldly popularity and power. The Nicolaitans taught that behavior did not matter. Balaam was a prophet of God who used his spiritual position for personal honor and riches (His record is found in Numbers 22, 23, and 24 and 31:8, 16; also 2 Pet. 2:15 and Jude 11). Rather than working for the people of God, he joined King Balak. Balaam wanted the honor an earthly government could give him.

Emperor Constantine desired to bring unity to the empire, so he gave Roman Christianity political power. This began the union of Christianity with the state. The weapon the church is to use is not political power; it is the Word of God, "the sword of His mouth." If the church is not faithful to the Bible, it falls.

The name "Thyatira" (Rev. 2:18–29) means "sacrifice of contrition." It represents that period in church history which has been called the "dark ages." During the Thyatira period of church history, state-supported Christianity embraced and enforced many pagan practices. Satan had succeeded in bringing in "Jezebel, who calls herself a prophetess" to corrupt Christianity. Jezebel was the daughter of the king of the Zidonians. Ahab, king of Israel, took her as his wife (see 1 Kings 16:31; chapters 18, 19, and 21; 2 Kings 9:7–37). She brought in hundreds of prophets of Baal to teach the people. She persecuted God's prophets. They had to go into hiding.

Revelation 12:6–15 tells us that Christ's faithful church was in the wilderness. What Paul warned about in 2 Thessalonians 2:2–7 had developed. "I gave her time to repent but she repented not." Over the centuries, voices were raised, pointing out the errors and calling for faithfulness to Christ. The call to repent climaxed in the Reformation. The Council of Trent made some reforms but said "no" to the claim that the Bible was the final authority for Christians. The "bed of sickness" and "death" could refer to the black plague, which is estimated to have killed one–fourth of the population of Europe, and also the ongoing religious wars following the Reformation (read C. Mervyn Maxwell's *God Cares*– vol. 2, pp. 125, 126).

The name "Sardis" (Rev. 3:1–6) means "that which remains; or the escape of the remnant". Sardis' mistake was to focus on the past. The Reformation had restored vital truth to Christianity. Sardis needed to continue to advance with God's work on earth. Her "deeds were not completed in the sight of God." The

Reformation was not completed. It needed to continue. If Sardis failed to recognize and advance with God's ongoing work of reform, then Jesus would "come like a thief and you will not know at what hour I will come upon you." Jesus spoke of the "end" and the "harvest of the earth" (Matt. 13:24–30, 36–43; 24; Luke 21:1–28). God's prophecies relating to the "last days" and the "time of the end" needed to be studied and understood. Daniel 8:14, with Revelation 10 and 14, reveal to us that "the hour of God's judgment is come" and Christ's coming is near.

The well-known meaning of "Philadelphia" (Rev. 3:7–13) is "brotherly love." He who is holy and true speaks to His church that has "kept His word." Bible societies had developed. Missionary work was emphasized. No reproof is given. Philadelphia, like its Lord and Savior, kept true to God's word. Out of love for God and people, they proclaimed heaven's word that the 2,300 years of Daniel 8:14 were ending. To them, the "cleansing of the Sanctuary, meant the return of Christ. They looked for and proclaimed Christ's appearing. In anticipation of the disappointment that came when Jesus did not then appear, Christ gave the assurance: "I am coming quickly." Those "who say they are Jews, and are not, but they lie" refer to Christians who opposed the prophetic message of Christ's return. They said the millennium was about to commence and the coming of Christ was far in the future.

Laodicea (Rev. 3:14–22) was a wealthy city. When an earthquake destroyed much of the city, the citizens refused the help offered by the emperor. They did not need help. There was nothing more comfortable than soaking in the warm springs nearby. Robes made from the black wool of their flocks were their mark of distinction. They also produced an eye medicine. "We need nothing."

The name means "judging of the people". Here is Christianity in "the time of the end", the last days. It should make us think of the lesson God gave in the annual "Day of Atonement." Revelation announces it with the words "the hour of God's judgment is come" (Rev. 14:6–12). Christianity is a respected faith and enjoying worldly prosperity (Smyrna was in poverty, but rich in Christ's eyes). Now, entire nations of the world regard themselves

The War Against Christ's Church and His Gospel

as "Christian." Large religious facilities are built. Christianity enjoys political influence. Western Christianity feels comfortable enjoying the ways of the world, but she is spiritually bankrupt. What is needed is for those who call themselves Christians to open their lives to Christ and have a real union with Him by studying and obeying His word.

Christ says to Laodicea, "to the person who overcomes will I grant to sit with Me on My throne." To Philadelphia, Christ said, "I am coming quickly." Laodicea, the "judging of the people", enables Him to "give to every person according to their works" when He comes to bring His family home. Come to Him and allow Him to prepare you for eternal life.

This study emphasizes that Christ gave warning that false ideas and practices would constantly seek to corrupt His gospel and church. The "falling away" occurred. Much of Christianity became corrupted. However, Christ has always had His people of faith. They "hear what the Spirit says" and have this as their mission: "This gospel of the kingdom shall be preached in all the world, for a witness unto all nations. Then shall the end come."

In the first four seals (6:1–8), more about the "falling away" of Christianity is revealed. We are to know these warnings and avoid them. However, we must remember that we are not called to focus on error. Christ is Savior and Lord. He is our focus. We are to witness to Him, His salvation, and ongoing heavenly ministry that guides His people and climaxes in His return to this earth. Constrained by His love and continual ministry for us, we experience the joy of His salvation now and anticipate the wonders of that which Christ has prepared for those who love Him.

These seven messages from Christ call each of His followers to "overcome." We overcome through faith "by the blood of the Lamb, and the word of our testimony" (Rev. 12:11). We "keep the commandments of God and hold to the testimony of Jesus." "Here is the perseverance of the saints who keep the commandments of God and their faith in Jesus" (Rev. 12:17; 14:12).

The Seven Seals Portray Christianity

Christ's followers—Christians— constitute God's kingdom on earth (see Matt. 3:2; 4:17; 24:14). In the first four seals (Rev. 6:1–8) is portrayed what occurred in Christianity as a kingdom. The four horsemen depict Christianity as a kingdom. The symbol of a rider on a horse portrays a leader with an organized following. As Christianity spread, it became a strong influence within the empire. It changed the society, but society also changed it. After Emperor Constantine had united Roman Christianity with the state, it grew into a powerful society that came to dominate Christianity in the Middle Ages.

When the Lamb broke the first seal, "John looked, and saw a white horse, the rider had a bow, and a crown was given to him, and he went out conquering and to conquer" (Rev. 6:1, 2). A white horse is a symbol of purity and victory. This depicts the apostles and followers of Jesus as they carried the good news to their world. Their pure witness to Christ changed the Roman Empire (R.A. Anderson, in *Unfolding the Revelation*, gives biblical and historical evidence for this). Elders were ordained in every church. Apostles' letters circulated among the churches, which cooperated in supporting each other (see Titus 1:5; Col. 4:16; Rom. 16:16; 1 Cor. 16: 1).

The second seal (Rev. 6:3, 4— A.D. 100–311) depicts a red horse—sin (see Isaiah 1:18; Rev. 12:3—red dragon; Rev. 17:4—scarlet woman). In Smyrna, the second church period, there was severe persecution and death. History reveals that not only were

Armageddon's Glorious End

there various persecutions of Christians, but during the second and third centuries, various Christian men arose with different teachings about Christ and His salvation (see Acts 20:30). They "fought" each other. The mystery of iniquity was at work with its error-causing strife among Christians.

The third Seal (Rev. 6:5, 6; A.D. 311–538) depicts a black horse. The light of the gospel was eclipsed. The rider holds a pair of balances. When Emperor Constantine officially established Roman Christianity, his judgment prevailed. He called Church Councils. He influenced and enforced their decisions. Christian leaders like "Balaam" (Rev. 2:14) cooperated with him. This fateful union of church and state continued for centuries.

The fourth seal (Rev. 6:7, 8; A.D. 538–1798) depicts a pale-horse, the color of death. "If the light that is in you be darkness, how great is that darkness" (Matt. 6:23). Christ's words fit the pale horse. Jezebel's work (fourth church, Rev. 2:20) brought pagan ideas and practices into official Christianity. The power of the state was used to enforce obedience. Many were labeled "heretics" and persecuted and put to death. Wars were waged to enforce the power of the official church. The gospel, which "is the power of God unto salvation", was made an instrument of persecution and death.

Why were there no horsemen associated with seals five, six, and seven? Following the Reformation, Christianity splintered and could no longer be pictured by a single horse or rider.

The fifth Seal (Rev. 6:9–11) depicts those who had been martyred for their witness to Christ. Jesus had foretold this in Matthew 24:21–22. The fifth seal also predicts the beginning of a pre-advent judgment (v. 11). Heaven reverses the earthly judgment. Judgment is given in favor of the saints (see Dan. 7:22). Though their faith and obedience were condemned by the state, it was a witness to the righteousness of Christ which covers them. "They must rest a little while longer." "Blessed are those who die in the Lord that they may rest from their labor, and their works follow them" (Rev. 14:13). Circumstances on earth made it appear that God had forsaken them. He had not. He sustained them in their witness, and their faithfulness inspires their Christian descendants to follow their example (see Deut. 32:43).

The Seven Seals Portray Christianity

The events of the fifth and sixth seals give evidence that the people of earth have come to the last days, the "time of the end" (see Dan. 8:17; 12:4; 10:14; 11:35). The events portrayed in the previous seals occurred over time, so the events the fifth and sixth seals occur over a period of time. From the Bible, we see that God gives warnings of coming judgments. Examples include Noah's flood, Sodom, and Jerusalem's destruction. Heaven sends the message: "that there should be delay no longer"; "the hour of His judgement has come" (Rev. 10:6; 14:7. NKJV).

Under the sixth seal (Rev. 6:12–17), awe-inspiring events occur in the natural world. Jesus spoke of such things (Matthew 24:29). They would occur after the "tribulation", which He prophesied in Matthew 24:29–31. Old Testament prophets had also spoken of such events. Natural disasters such as the Lisbon earthquake, the "Dark Day" in New England, and the unrivaled star shower of 1833 caused people to think about and study Bible prophecy. Out of that study came an urgent conviction that Christ's coming was at hand and the world must be told to prepare for that great and wonderful event (depicted in Rev. 10). The events pictured in the sixth seal end with the second coming of Christ and the terror of the wicked at His appearing. The prophecy presents us with the great question: "Who shall be able to stand?" (This echoes Zeph. 1:14–18; Mal. 3:2; Isa. 33:14).

This pivotal question is answered in Revelation 7. God has His people. They are pictured as 12,000 men from each of the twelve tribes of Israel who are "sealed in their foreheads." God's promises have not failed. The victorious "Son of David" has provided victory. Because they are Christ's, they constitute the Israel of God. They receive the promises (Gal. 3:28, 29). The 144,000 depicted in Revelation 7:4–10 appear again in 14:1–5. That is after the issuing of the death threat for not worshipping the way the beast commands (Rev. 13:11–17). Their acceptance of and faithfulness to the messages of Revelation 14:6–12 is what sealed them. Revelation 12:17 says that they "keep the commandments of God and have the testimony of Jesus Christ." The keeping of God's commandments identifies them as Christ's new-covenant people. God has written His Law in their hearts and minds (see Heb. 8:8–10; 10:9–16). Because they are sealed, they are protected during the plagues and the judgment of Revelation 19:11–21.

How shall we understand the number, 144,000? It is small when compared to the billions of people on earth. It is God's number. Twelve appears as God's symbolic kingdom number, twelve tribes, twelve Apostles, twelve gates of the new Jerusalem. For those who hold to a literalness it is helpful to remember that biblical numbering counted men, leaving uncounted all the women and children who were also present. Revelation 21:12–14 tells us that there are twelve gates for the New Jerusalem. On the gates are the names of the twelve tribes, so all who enter are counted as associated with the twelve tribes, yet on the foundations are the names of the twelve apostles of the Lamb—Christ's called leaders.

> *Heaven still speaks. Christ, at the throne of God as our Mediator, speaks for us and to us.*

The seventh seal (Rev. 8:1) depicts "silence in heaven for about half an hour" (a more thorough explanation of this can be found in the Appendix). What does this mean? God, from the beginning, has been in communication with the human race. After Adam's sin, God came asking, "Where are you (I have saving news for you)" (Gen. 2:15, 16; 3:8, 9, 15)? God spoke through the prophets. Finally, He spoke through His Son (see Heb. 1:1, 2). There on Patmos, the Son, by His Spirit, spoke to John and all Christians.

Heaven still speaks. Christ, at the throne of God as our Mediator, speaks for us and to us. "The Spirit and the bride say, Come." "Today, hear His voice and harden not your hearts."

God's Sealing Work (Revelation 7:1-3)

Revelation 6 closed with the question: "who shall be able to stand?" God's sealing work answers that question. God will have a people who can stand before Him when "the great day of His wrath comes." In that glorious and awful day, His people will "shine with brightness (see Dan. 12).

"This sealing is a pledge from God of perfect security to His chosen ones. Sealing indicates that you are God's chosen. He has appropriated you to Himself. As the sealed of God, we are Christ's purchased possession, no one shall pluck us out of His hands" (E.G. White, *Christ Triumphant*, p. 10)

It is true that all who in faith accept Jesus as their Savior, giving themselves to God by baptism, are sealed with the Holy Spirit (see 2 Cor. 1:22; Eph. 1:13, 14; 4:30). God's end-time seal is a seal of deliverance, as was the blood on the doorposts of the houses of God's people during that first Passover when they were delivered from Egypt. It is placed on the foreheads of God's servants by the angels during the final test of faith.

This sealing in Revelation 7 is similar to the mark of deliverance given in the vision of Ezekiel 9 and 10. Our long-suffering God did all He could to turn Israel back to Him. God is not anxious to pour out His wrath and destroy all unbelievers (read Ezekiel 33:11; 18:23, 32; 2 Peter 3:9, 10). The Scriptures reveal that He gives warning of coming judgment. It is evident in the flood story. He warned Egypt, Nineveh, Israel, and Judah of coming judgment. Revelation 14:7 speaks to us today; it tells us that "the hour of

Armageddon's Glorious End

His judgment is come." World events continue in the direction foretold in Scripture.

In this vision, John saw four angels holding winds of strife and destruction. Another angel ascends from the east, commanding them to continue to restrain the winds till "we have sealed the servants of our God on their foreheads." Then John "heard the number of those who were sealed. 144,000 of all the tribes of the children of Israel were sealed." There were 12,000 from each of the twelve tribes named. John did not see the twelve tribes. When he turned to look, he saw a great multitude which could not be counted of all nations, people, and languages (The 144,000 appear again in chapter 14; more information is given there).

One might wonder why the twelve tribes are named when the nation had ceased to exist as composed of twelve tribes. Assyria had displaced the ten northern tribes (723/22 B.C.). They appear no more in history. The promises given to Israel and the prophecies of Ezekiel 40–48 are no doubt the reason. Ezekiel was taken to Babylon (597 B.C.). Daniel and his group had been there at least eight years. In 586 B.C., Babylonian armies returned, and this time Jerusalem was destroyed. That was not to be the end of the Jewish nation. God had a mission for them to fulfill. The visions given through Ezekiel pictured what the Lord would do, provided they would be true to Him. Ezekiel 48 lists the future open to the twelve tribes. The naming of the tribes by John reveals that the prophecies of God are all ultimately fulfilled through Christ. The prophecy of Daniel 9:24–27 helps us see this.

Daniel's great concern for his people and Holy City led him to fast and pray on their behalf. The vision revealed that Jerusalem would be rebuilt. The Jewish nation was given "seventy sevens"—490 years to fulfill the purpose God had for them. Messiah would come. He would solve the sin problem and bring in everlasting righteousness. Perplexed, and with great sadness, Daniel also wrote that the city would again be destroyed.

Jesus the Messiah came at the prophesied time. After three and a half years, He was officially rejected by the leaders of the nation. On that Palm Sunday, as Jesus approached the city, He wept over it. He said, "if you in this your day had known the things

God's Sealing Work (Revelation 7:1–3)

that make for your peace! but now they are hidden from your eyes" (Luke 19:41–44). Israel was called to be God's servant. They were to be God's light on the earth. "I will make you a name and praise among all people of the earth" (Zeph. 3:20). Theirs was to be a reputation and glory greater than that of King Solomon's early years.

The next day, teaching in the temple, Christ told the parable of the vineyard owner who left his vineyard in the care of his servants. At vintage time, he sent his servants for the fruits of the vineyard. The caretakers of the vineyard beat and stoned those who were sent. The owner sent more, and they were also rejected. At last, he sent his son, saying, "they will respect my son." "The caretakers of the vineyard said, let us kill him and take over the vineyard for our own." Then Jesus asked the chief priests and elders, "What will the owner do to his caretakers when he comes to his vineyard?"

Their answer was, "He will destroy those wicked men. He will lease his vineyard to others who will give him the fruits when harvested." Responding to their judgment, Christ said, "Therefore I say to you, the kingdom of God will be taken from you and given to a nation bearing the fruits of it" (Matthew 21:33-43).

On His last day in the temple as a faithful prophet, He spoke "woe" upon all those leaders of the people who had decided and planned to have Him killed. He ended with the words of Matthew 23:37–39. He had prayed and worked so earnestly to gather them back to God, "but you were not willing. Your house is left to you desolate."

The New Testament presents to us the true Israel of God. All the promises of God come to people in and through Jesus Christ (2 Cor. 1:20). They do not belong to one single race. "If you are Christ's, you are Abraham's seed and heirs according to the promise." "For as many of you were baptized into Christ, have put on Christ. There is neither Jew nor Greek, there is neither slave nor free, there is neither male nor female; for you are all one in Christ." (Gal. 3:14, 29, 27, 28).

An example of God's sealing work comes from the first Passover. In Exodus 12, God told the people what they were to do to be safe in His care. It was more than having the blood of a slain lamb placed on the door posts of each dwelling. The people must first believe that their deliverance was at hand and be prepared for the journey. They were to have food prepared to go. All the preparation was a manifestation that they believed God's word. They were settled in God's truth for them. The people were sealed by faith that obeyed, putting blood on the door and being within their home.

The angel that announces God's sealing work "ascends from the east." He is not described as coming down from heaven, but ascending as the sun arises. It pictures his sealing message as beginning from darkness but growing brighter and brighter until its light covers the world, as pictured in Revelation 18:1.

The message God uses for His sealing work is found in Revelation 14:6–12. The three messages bring the world to the climax of the gospel of Jesus Christ. The messages result in the harvest of the earth.

The Lord will finally allow what the majority of people desire. The restraining power of God will be removed. People will be free to do whatever they feel like doing. The winds of passion, strife, and violence will be loosed. Natural disasters and tornadoes of human desire, anger, and greed, will devastate all of society (see E.G. White, *Christ Triumphant*, p. 102).

The Seven Trumpets

Revelation 8:2–11:18

Trumpets first appear in Scripture at Mount Sinai. God used the sound of a trumpet to assemble the people to hear Him speak (Ex. 19:16–19). Later, the Lord instructed Moses to make two silver trumpets which were used to call an assembly to seek the Lord, or to sound an alarm (Num. 10:1–10).

The Lord, in His appeal through the prophet Joel, said, "Blow the trumpet in Zion, sound an alarm...Turn to Me with all your heart...Blow the trumpet in Zion, sanctify a fast, call a solemn assembly". All were to seek the Lord (Joel 2:1, 12–17; Zeph. 2:14–17; 2:1–3). The conflicts and apostasy within Christianity led those who held to the pure gospel and prayed earnestly for grace to remain faithful (Rev. 8:3, 4).

To Sound the Alarm of War and Disaster

The fall of Jericho was signaled by trumpets (see Josh. 6:3). The trumpets sounded by Gideon's army signaled defeat and devastation of the Midianites (Judges 6:16–18). Jeremiah cried out in great distress, "because he had heard the sound of the trumpet, the alarm of war. Destruction upon destruction is cried" (Jer. 4:19–21, 5; 6:1). In Jeremiah 42:14, we are told that the remnant in Judah disobeyed God's instruction and was determined to go to Egypt, believing that in Egypt they would "see no war, nor hear the sound of the trumpet", but trumpets and war did follow them there.

The sounding of the seven trumpets of Revelation signal disaster, destruction, and war. Highly symbolic language is used to describe the events signaled by the trumpets: "Hail, fire, worm wood, blood, locusts, burning mountain, star," etc. Such language was used by the ancient prophets as they spoke of war and God's judgments (see Deut. 29:18; Jer. 9:14, 15; Isa. 7:4; 28:2; Ezekiel 5:1–4, 12; 38:22; Joel 1:4, 6, 7; 2:3, 4; Amos 5:6, 7; Nahum 3:14–17). As the Old Testament symbolism referred primarily to the disaster and distress brought by invading armies, so the trumpets of Revelation refer to the same type of events (R.A. Anderson's *Unfolding Revelation* and Uriah Smith's *Daniel And Revelation* give excellent explanations of events depicted by the trumpets. *God Cares* by C. Mervyn Maxwell is also helpful).

This cursory look at the trumpets is to note their effect on the gospel and Christianity. The first four trumpets signal events that caused the breakup of the Roman Empire. In them is depicted how the "legs of Iron" of the image of Daniel 2 became divided into the "feet and toes" that make up the nations of Europe. These events enabled the "blasphemous little horn" of Daniel 7 to rise to power [the dragon gave him his seat, power, and great authority (Rev. 13:2–6)]

First trumpet: Alaric and the Goths, A.D. 395 to the sack of Rome in A.D. 410.

Second trumpet: A maritime war by Genseric and the Vandals. In A.D. 455, he sailed into the mouth of the Tiber, destroyed 1,100 Roman ships, and pillaged the city.

Third trumpet: Invasion by Attila and the Huns.

Fourth trumpet: Sun, moon, and stars are smitten. "In 476 A.D. Odoacer, the chief of a barbarian remnant of Attila, declared that the name and office of the Roman emperor in the West be abolished. The Senate bowed in submission, and so Romulus Augustulus, the last of the Roman rulers was dethroned. Thus the 'sun' of the empire had set. The 'moon' and the 'stars' -the counsels and senate-lingered a little longer, but before another half century had passed, these too were extinguished" (R.A. Anderson, *Unfolding the Revelation*, p. 89).

These invasions resulted in many pagan practices being incorporated into Roman Christianity. This power vacuum enabled the Bishop of Rome to rise in authority and dominate Christianity. The church claimed control of the salvation which

The Seven Trumpets

Christ has provided. The ministry of human priests replaced the ministry of Christ at the throne of God.

The fifth, sixth, and seventh trumpets are called "woe" trumpets (Rev. 8:13; 9:12; 11:14; 10:7; 11:15). What makes them "woes?" It is because they signal the emergence of belief systems that become rivals to faith in Christ. These belief systems war against the gospel, Bible, and God Himself. Without the gospel of Christ, people are left in darkness and woe. The fifth and sixth trumpets signal the rise of the religion of Islam and the Muslim nations. This resulted in the Christian faith being blotted out in many areas and brought an end to the Eastern Roman Empire. This further enhanced the Bishop of Rome.

During the period of the sixth trumpet, a new humanistic faith emerged to challenge God centered faith. It developed out of what is called "The Enlightenment." It is shown in the vision of Revelation 11:7–14. These verses apply to the French Revolution in which reason was deified and Christianity condemned. The church, combined with the state, had been so oppressive that the only way to have liberty was to get rid of the church. This occurred again in the Russian Revolution. The Czar and church had been so oppressive that the revolution turned against religious faith.

The "Enlightenment" had contributed to this. It had exalted human reason and negated faith in God. This naturalism gave a new way to interpret the physical world and life. It is the basis for the theory of evolution. It has become the dominant influence in philosophy, ethics, and theology. It turns people away from God and His Word. It makes Christ and His life into nothing more than a nice human story. This work of Satan is more effective for his purposes than keeping the Bible away from people. From below, out of the abyss, Satan has flooded the world with his wisdom (see Rev. 9:1, 2, 11).

The book *Education* (published 1903) contains the following comment by E.G. White: "The world-wide dissemination of the same teachings that led to the French Revolution all are tending to involve the whole world in a struggle similar to that which convulsed France" (p. 228). The rise of atheistic Communism speaks to the fulfillment of her words. Calling the ideas "naturalism" does not make them less atheistic.

Today's popular culture ascribes no respect or authority to Jesus Christ and His gospel. Christianity is regarded as one religion among many which a person may choose or ignore. Without Christ, life has no meaning, and we have no future. It is no wonder that the Bible calls these developments "woes" for the human race.

Revelation 12–14 give us another group of visions which expand our understanding of prophecy. It is the events of Revelation 13:12–17 that constitute the third woe. Before we get to those chapters, we have chapters 10 and 11. Revelation 10 depicts God's work for the world as the 2,300 day/year period comes to its close. Earth has entered Daniel's "time of the end", the "last days", and climax of the gospel.

Heaven's Warning Message to Earth (Revelation 10)

Verse 1—A mighty being comes down from heaven. He is "clothed with a cloud." Clouds are a token of Christ and His deity. Jesus returned to heaven "in a cloud." "Behold He comes with clouds" "One like the Son of Man came with the clouds of heaven" (Ex. 19:9; Acts 1:9; Rev. 1:7; Dan. 7:13).

"A rainbow was upon his head." In the vision of God's throne (4:3), there was a rainbow around it. Ezekiel saw the same thing in his vision (Ezek. 1:28). The rainbow is a sign of God's covenant of deliverance and His restraining power over the earth as He works to bring people to repentance and salvation.

"His face was as the sun, His feet as pillars of fire." This is the description given in Revelation 1:15-16. This is the "messenger of the covenant," the One of whom Jacob spoke as "the angel that redeemed me" (Mal. 3:1; Gen. 48:16—"angel" or "messenger" are translated from the same Hebrew or Greek word).

Verse 2—"He set His right foot on the sea and His left foot on the earth." This position denotes His supreme power and authority over the whole world. When Jesus commissioned His disciples, he said, "all power in heaven and earth is given to Me…" all things have been put under the feet of Christ (Matt. 28:18; 1 Cor. 15:27).

It is the authority of Christ Himself that gives and stands behind the message that is brought to earth in Revelation 10. He holds in His hand a "little book." The "little book" is opened.

Armageddon's Glorious End

The book has not always been open. The scene and these words recall Daniel 12:7–10. Daniel was told that some of the words he wrote were sealed until the time of the end. Then "the wise would understand." This message ushered our world into "the time of the end," the "last days."

Verses 3 and 4—"He cried with a loud voice as when a lion roars." Have you heard a lion roar? I remember being at the Philadelphia Zoo, by the lion house, and for the first time in my life, I heard a lion roar. It was a deep, reverberating sound. I felt the vibrations. It surely catches one's attention. It caught John's attention. He sees this mighty being. He hears His loud commanding voice. Then he hears seven thunders speak. He was going to write what the seven thunders said, but a voice from heaven said, "don't write what the thunders said."

Verses 5–7—John watched as the mighty, heavenly being took an oath and spoke. This is a God-given message for the world. The message came from Him who exists forever and created heaven, earth, the sea, and all that is in them. This message describes events on earth that occurred as the 2,300 days/years of Daniel 8:14 were ending ("Time no more shall be" is the literal meaning of the Greek. Some versions of the Bible use the word "delay" instead of "time". The Greek word means "time". Of the thirty appearances of this word, this is the only place where "delay" has been substituted for "time". See Maxwell, *God Cares*, pp. 304, 305).

The gospel has an end. It is reaching its climax. Jesus and His apostles taught it. It has been proclaimed "by all His holy prophets since the world began." It is brought about by the return of Christ to this world (Acts 3:19–21). "The mystery of God should be finished." What is this mystery? It is the good news of salvation as presented in the gospel of Jesus Christ (see Rom. 16:25; Eph. 6:19; Col. 4:3).

"The mystery of God has been called, 'God's scheme of redemption;' 'the eschatological mystery of the world's history;' 'the glorious completion of the divine kingdom;' Mystery is used because the world does not see and know what God is really doing through the course of the ages. Mystery implies that we ourselves

Heaven's Warning Message to Earth (Revelation 10)

do not know except by a revelation which God has supplied. The church has this revelation and walks in its light" (R.C.H. Lenski, *Interpretation of St. John's Revelation*. p. 319).

We could not know that we are living in the end time of this world's history except that God has revealed it by His prophetic word. Fulfilled prophecy establishes where we are in history. Revelation 10 depicts God's work in the earth as the 2,300 day/year prophecy of Daniel 8:14 was ending. It ushered in "the time of the end" (Dan. 8:17, 19; 11:35, 40; 12:4, 9, 13; 2:28; 10:14).

Jesus spoke of time given to the nations of the earth to see what they would do with Christ and His gospel (see Luke 21:24. Matt. 24:14). Daniel 9:23–27 tells us that "70 weeks", the first 490 years of the 2,300 day/year prophecy, were given to the Jews that they might fulfill God's purpose for them as His nation. They refused and "did not know the time of their visitation" (Luke 19:41–44; Matt. 21:42, 43; Acts 13:46–48). As for the Jewish nation, so for the gentile nations of the earth. They have their time to respond to God and His Christ or confirm their rebellion against God and His law. The mystery of God is about to be completed. "Behold He comes with clouds and every eye will see Him" (Rev. 1:7).

The eighteenth century brought new life into Christianity ("The Great Awakening"). Missionary societies and Bible societies were formed. There was an awakening to the words of Christ: "I will come again." Political events, especially the French Revolution, with its atheism, stimulated the study of Bible prophecy. Prophetic conferences were held in England. The 1,260 days/forty-two months/time, times, and half a time of Daniel and Revelation were seen as fulfilled. The 2,300 days/years of Daniel were seen to be ending.

Le Roy E. Froom, in his four-volume work *The Prophetic Faith of Our Fathers*, lists 150 Bible scholars who ended the 2,300 day/year prophecy in the 1840s. They used the instruction given to Moses and to Ezekiel (that a "day" in the prophecy equaled a year in fulfillment—Num. 34:14; Ezek. 4:6) (*The Prophetic Faith of Our Fathers*, Vol, III, pp. 744, 745; vol. IV, pp. 404, 405).

The day-equaling-a-year principle is certainly evident in the prophecies of Daniel 7, 8, and 9. Daniel did not understand what he had been shown (see 8:27). He was aware that Jeremiah's prophetic word said Israel would be captive to Babylon for seventy years. He prayed for understanding (see 9:1–22). The angel Gabriel was sent to give him understanding. The seventy weeks of Daniel 9:24–27, as fulfilled in the life of Christ, clearly show that a day equaling a year is the key to understanding the prophecy.

Thus, many Bible scholars agreed that the "two-thousand three hundred days" meant years. There were some differences as to when they began, but most ended them in the 1840s. There were significant differences as to what "then shall the sanctuary be cleansed (made right)" indicated. The most common understanding was that it referred to Christ's return to earth in power and glory. This was the message that was proclaimed and reached its climax in 1844.

His message is "Time no more shall be, in the days of the voice of the seventh angel when he shall begin to sound, the mystery of God is finished, as He has preached to His servants the prophets." The "time of the end", the climax of the gospel, has come.

John was told to take and eat the open book. A delightful sweetness came from eating the book, but then it turned to bitterness. This was the experience of those who embraced the truth that the 2,300 years of Daniel 8:14 were ending in 1844. Christian history calls it the Millerite Movement. The message went everywhere. With great joy, people looked for the return of Jesus. That was sweet. When He did not appear, it was very bitter. The vision closes with the words: "You must prophesy again before many people." This was a puzzle, for if the vision meant the return of Jesus, there could be no more preaching.

In their disappointment, God's people of faith prayed and studied together. The Holy Spirit led them to do what Revelation 11:1 tells them to do: "rise and measure the temple of God which is in heaven." They found no biblical support that this earth was God's sanctuary to be cleansed. God's true temple is in heaven. The book of Revelation has nineteen references to the temple, tabernacle, or altar in the heavenly sanctuary. They found that Jesus Christ, our Great High Priest and Mediator at the throne of God, then entered into His "Day of Atonement" ministry. It would prepare His people of faith for His return. The "prophesying again" that His people must do is given in Revelation 14:6–12. Then the harvest of the earth occurs (14:14–20).

The bitter experience of Revelation 10 is similar to what Christ's disciples experienced during the week of His crucifixion. By His Psalm Sunday, triumphal procession, they felt sure Christ was about to assume authority and destroy Roman rule. Instead, by Friday, He was on the cross. What a bitter disappointment was theirs! Following the resurrection of Christ, they were brought to see the necessity of His suffering and death. They came to understand that God's Messiah did not come to bring political exaltation to the Jews. He came to provide salvation and redemption for all humanity.

Up to that time, no one connected the vision of Revelation 10 with the end of the 2,300 day/year prophecy. It was only afterward that the application was seen, with the words of verse 11—"you must prophesy again"—becoming the mission before them.

Read in the following books: *God Cares*, vol. 2, by C. Mervyn Maxwell, pp. 274–280; *The Great Controversy* by E.G. White, the chapter, 'An American Reformer", p. 317; *Unfolding The Revelation* by R.A. Anderson, Chapter 10, p. 97 (It was not William Miller who set the October 22 date. He was one of the last to accept it. He spoke only of the year, not the day. That date was set by another man).

Light from God's Temple in Heaven

Revelation 11 continues the vision of chapter 10. It begins with the instruction to "measure the temple of God, the altar, and those who worship in it." "Measuring the temple" called for Christians to understand the gospel lessons taught by the temple with its daily and yearly round of sacrifice and ceremony. This was necessary for the "prophesying again" commanded in Revelation 10:11 and would also give the reason for the "bittersweet" experience of those involved in "eating the little book."

The earthly temple, with its yearly services, symbolically portrayed God's great work for the redemption of humanity. God's redemptive work does more than provide personal salvation. It solves the problem of sin for the universe. It is Christ's continual ministry in heaven, symbolized by the altar of intercession, which enables God's work on earth and leads to the time when the problem of sin will be settled by God's righteous judgment. "Leave out the court..."—The various offerings made in the courtyard were fulfilled by "the offering of Jesus Christ, once for all." He was the Lamb which God supplied. Jesus was born in the courtyard of this world. In His human nature, He overcame all sin and Satan, then He took all our sin upon Himself and died in our place. When He cried "It is finished", salvation changed from being a promise into reality. "Graves opened." "Now, salvation, and strength, and the kingdom of our God, and the power of His Christ have come..." (Matt. 27:51–53; Rev. 12:10). Satan had no more standing in heaven. All of his efforts are now directed against the gospel and church, to keep people lost.

The "measuring of the temple and its worshippers" was to bring Christians back to the understanding of where we are to look for salvation. Do we look to a church, priests, and the sacraments, or directly to Christ in His heavenly ministry (Heb. 12:2, 22–28; Phil. 1:6; 1 John 1:9)? Christians had applied Daniel 8:14 as leading to Christ's return to earth rather than to the beginning of His "judgment hour" ministry in the temple in heaven (see Rev. 14:7). Failure to correctly apply the words "and then shall the sanctuary be cleansed" (Dan. 8:14) to Christ's ministry in heaven is the reason why the "sweet" experience in Revelation 10 became "bitter." Many verses in Revelation call us back to the reality that it is Christ and His continual ministry in heaven that brings His salvation to us (11:1, 2, 19; 8:3, 4; 14:15, 17; 15:5, 6; 16:1, 7, 17; see also John 14:6; Rom. 8:34; Heb. 4:14–16; 7:25). Our salvation comes only through "Christ, at the throne of God for us." (Acts 4:12; Heb. 9:24).

God's redemptive work does more than provide personal salvation. It solves the problem of sin for the universe.

Christ and the apostles warned that false Christs and prophets would arise to lead people away from the gospel and His saving ministry. It would climax in "the man of sin sitting in the temple of God", claiming the prerogatives of God (2 Thess. 2:3–8). The scholars who produced the King James Bible, in their introduction to it, interpreted, "the man of sin," as applying to the papal system.

Contrast the Bible truth of Christ's ministry in heaven with the claims and teaching of the "little horn power" of Daniel 7 and 8. The horn power would throw down the truth and heavenly sanctuary. The vital, necessary intercession of Christ at the throne of God has been replaced by the ministry of priests, tradition, and church sacraments.

Our salvation is not based on what human priests may do. We do not look to Rome or Jerusalem. "There is One Mediator between God and man, the Man Christ Jesus." "If anyone sin we have an Advocate with the Father, Jesus Christ the righteous."

Light from God's Temple in Heaven

"We come boldly to the throne of grace to obtain mercy" (1 Tim. 2:5; Heb. 4:16. 1 John 2:1). "Jesus is able to save completely, those who come to God by Him, seeing he ever lives to make intercession for them." "Christ died, rose again, is at the right hand of God making intercession for us" (John 14:6, 13, 14, 19; Acts 2:33; Rom. 8:34; Heb. 7:25). Christ's "one offering" for sin is sufficient for all salvation (Heb. 9:12, 25–28; 10:10).

In addition to the temple, God's two witnesses and the forty-two month/1,260 day/year prophetic period are brought to view in Revelation 11:2–3. This period is mentioned twice in Daniel's prophecies and five times in Revelation. It was during that period that the "little horn" power of Daniel 7 and 8 dominated and changed the gospel. That power ignored the continual ministry of Christ in heaven (Dan. 8:10–14). It taught that in order to receive God's grace, believers were dependent upon the ministry of human priests. Christ's ministry in the heavenly temple was obscured.

It was during that same prophetic time that "God's two witnesses prophesied clothed in sackcloth" and His woman of Revelation 12 was sheltered in the wilderness. Who or what are the two witnesses? Jesus appointed His church to be His witness to all the earth (Matt. 28:19, 20; Luke 24:46–49; Acts 1:8). His church is to live and proclaim His gospel. The Bible is the other witness.

The Scripture was always given as a witness for God. "Hear the word of the Lord." "You err, not knowing the Scriptures." "The Holy Scriptures are able to make you wise unto salvation." Jesus said, "Thy word is truth." He used Scripture as His truth and defense. He warned against changing in any way what He gave John to write (Rev. 22:16, 18, 19). Scripture, as taught and empowered by the Holy Spirit, is the authority for His church.

The seven churches reveal how, over the centuries, error continued to infiltrate Christian practice. What the Ephesus Church refused was found to be accepted in the Pergamos period. Following this, Thyatira is described as more pagan than Christian. Christ's church, which is composed of those who heeded His counsel to the churches and stayed faithful to Him, was condemned. No wonder it is pictured as clothed in sackcloth.

Armageddon's Glorious End

When Emperor Constantine legalized Christianity and then united it to his government, many people joined Christianity. They brought their old ways with them. Two centuries later, Emperor Justinian decreed that the Bishop of Rome was to be the head over all the churches. Roman Christianity was in apostasy. When that Decree of Justinian went into effect, the 1,260 day/year prophecy began (A.D. 538; It ended in 1798 when the pope was made a prisoner and exiled from Rome).

As the forty-two months/1,260 days/years referred to in 11:2–3 were closing, there is presented Satan's success in making war against God and His Word (Rev. 11:3–12). It is known as the French Revolution, in which reason was deified and the Bible and religion condemned (Many authors have documented the events of the French Revolution, which show how it fits the prophetic description of Revelation 11:2–14. See R.A. Anderson, *Unfolding The Revelation*, p. 109; C. Mervyn Maxwell, *God Cares*, vol. 2 pp. 186–93; E.G. White, *The Great Controversy*, chapter, "The Bible and the French Revolution", p. 265; Uriah Smith, *Daniel And Revelation*, pp. 281–9).

The French Revolution was like an earthquake to the nation. It destroyed the rule of kings. France became a republic. In 1804, the British and Foreign Bible Society was formed. The Bible became the most circulated book in the world and received great respect and honor. The war against the Bible and those who teach its truth continues. The teachings that led to the French Revolution have spread throughout the world. Scientific theories are used to discredit it and those who believe and teach it.

In France, the union of the church and the royal government had become so oppressive that the only way to have personal freedom was to destroy them both. The "Reign of Terror" resulted. The same situation was true regarding the Russian Revolution of 1917. Religion and freedom were seen as enemies of the people. Atheism resulted.

The opposite was the case in the establishment of the United States. God is recognized as the Giver of individual freedom. The Declaration of Independence declares that "all men are created equal, that they are endowed by their Creator with certain

Light from God's Temple in Heaven

unalienable Rights, that among these are Life, Liberty, and the Pursuit of Happiness." The two principles of religious freedom and political freedom are what have made America great.

Revelation 11:15–18 gives a description of the end of present-world history and the rejoicing in heaven over the event. The vision which began in Revelation 10:1 closes with "the temple of God opened in heaven, and there was seen in His temple the ark of His covenant." This opening of the temple in heaven calls Christians to focus on Christ's ministry there. Studying it brings a new understanding concerning final events in this fallen world's story. Chapters 21 and 22 give a teasing description of the new earth.

Revelation 11:1 names the temple, altar, and worshippers. They refer to the Holy Place of the sanctuary where the continuous, daily service took place. Verse 19 moves to the Most Holy Place, where the Ark of the Covenant was kept. Only once a year, on the Day of Atonement, was the Most Holy Place entered. The Day of Atonement ceremony was a reminder of the certainty of God's final judgment. The judgment is good news for God's people. The time of God's judgment was longed for by "the souls under the altar" (Rev. 6:9–11). The first of the three heaven-sent messages of Revelation 14:6–12 tells us to "Fear God and give glory to Him, for the hour of His judgment has come."

This view of the ark of the covenant has a greater message than reminding Christians of God's coming judgment. The ark contains God's law, the Ten Commandments. Revelation 12:17 and 14:12 tell us that His faithful people "keep the commandments of God." They love Jesus and have embraced His new covenant. God's law is written in their hearts and minds. His grace causes the "righteousness of the law to be fulfilled in us who walk not after the flesh, but after the Spirit (John 14:15; Heb. 8:6–10; 10:16; Rom. 8:3, 4). When James wrote, "So speak and so do as they that shall be judged by the law of liberty", He was referring to the Ten Commandments (James 2:10–12). This truth about God's law is included in the "prophesying again" of Revelation 10:11. These two chapters give Christians much to consider in knowing and serving God.

Armageddon's Glorious End

Revelation 11:18 states that judgment has been decided and is about to be executed. This is the transition point in the book of Revelation. From today's point of view, chapters 1–11 are a prophetic view of past Christian history. They are history described by the seven churches, seals, and trumpets.

Chapters 13–22 reveal final events in Satan's war against Christ's people (12:17), his defeat, and the earth made new. It is interesting to note that "ancient writings depict a war between the gods and a dragon of chaos (abyss)." They also refer to a seven-headed dragon (see *Seventh-day Adventist Bible Commentary*, vol. 4, on Isaiah 27:1, and vol. 8, p. 668, "Leviathan"). Revelation 12 makes the transition from Christian history to eschatology, which is the branch of theology dealing with last things such as death, resurrection, and the end of the world.

The Prominence of the Temple of God in the Book of Revelation

Revelation reveals that heaven's temple is the control center for God's work of salvation here on earth. The constant references throughout the chapters make evident our need to understand Christ's ministry in heaven's temple as it relates to His church and its work on earth (see Matthew 24:14).

Chapters 1–9 have the following references that remind us of the sanctuary or temple:

Rev. 1:4, 12, 20—The seven candlesticks (lampstands).

Rev. 3:12—"A pillar in the temple of my God."

Rev. 6:9–11—Souls under the altar cry out to God, asking Him to judge and make things right. Killed for their faith, as was the first martyr, Abel, their blood like his (Genesis 4:10) cries to God for justice to be done.

Rev. 7:9, 14, 15—Those who came through great tribulation before His throne, which is in the temple (Rev. 16:17; Psalm 11:4).

Rev. 8:2–5—The golden altar with its burning incense. It symbolizes Jesus, "who ever lives to make intercession for us" (Heb. 7:25; Rom. 8:34). It is Christ's heavenly intercession that presents our prayers to the Father and by which His answers come.

Rev. 9:13—A voice from the golden alter.

Revelation 11 begins with a command to measure the temple in heaven. It ends with the opening of the holy of holies revealing the ark of God's covenant (vs. 1, 2, 19).

Armageddon's Glorious End

Rev. 13:6—The beast blasphemes God and His tabernacle.

Rev. 14:15—An angel comes out of the temple, saying it is time to harvest the earth.

Rev. 14:17—Another angel out of the temple with a sharp sickle.

Rev. 14:18—Another angel came out from the altar, telling the angel of verse 17 to harvest the vine of the earth.

Rev. 15:5, 6—The temple of the tabernacle of testimony in heaven was opened. Out of the temple came the seven angels who had the seven plagues.

Rev. 15:8—The temple was filled with smoke from the glory of God and His power. "No one was able to enter the temple." God's time for salvation ended (see Heb. 6:18–20).

Rev. 16:1—A voice from the temple instructing the seven angels to go and pour out their plagues on the earth.

Rev. 16:7—Another voice from the altar saying true and right are Your judgments.

Rev. 16:17—After the seventh plague is poured out, a loud voice comes out of the temple from the throne saying, "It is done." The greatest earthquake in all history occurs and giant hailstones fall.

Rev. 21:3—"Behold the tabernacle of God is with men. He will dwell with them..." John saw no temple in the New Jerusalem (v. 22). "The Lord God Almighty and the Lamb are its temple."

A Woman, Her Child and the Dragon (Revelation 12)

Revelation 12 is vital for a correct world view and true philosophy of history. The seventeen verses recap Lucifer's great war against God, which is playing itself out here on planet earth. It sets the stage for the final events between Christ and Satan. The vision moves back and forth between God's saving work and Satan's work to prevent it.

The chapter opens with a gripping scene of a woman clothed with the sun and a garland of twelve stars on her head. She is in the pains of child birth (vs. 1, 2). She is the woman of Genesis 3:15 and represents God's people of faith who, through the centuries, looked for the promised "seed" who would crush the head of the serpent.

Verse 5 begins to give meaning to what is seen. Verses 7–9 expand our understanding. Satan's war against God had started "in heaven." He was already working against God at Creation. He was successful in tempting Eve to disobedience, after which Adam followed suit. Satan became prince of this world in place of Adam. The war that began in heaven became centered on earth. Most of earth's people follow him.

The woman who is clothed with the sun, moon under her feet, and a crown of twelve stars on her head, represents "the daughter of Zion", God's people of faith, "the bride of Christ"—His church (see Jer. 6:2; Gal. 3:7, 9; 2 Cor. 11:2). She looked and longed for the birth of the promised One (see Gen. 3:15). The present biblical application makes her to represent God's true church.

The "great red dragon" is Satan (verse 9). One-third of the angels followed him in his rebellion against God. The heads and horns indicate the governments and agencies through which he has worked in his efforts to frustrate Heaven's work of redemption.

The "man-child" is Jesus. By the life He lived, Christ overcame all sin and defeated Satan. By His death, He made it possible for all sinners to be forgiven and restored to God. By His life and death, all the allegations that Satan made against God were demonstrated to be false. Our salvation is no longer just a promise. It became a reality. His resurrection and ascension to God's throne proclaim the victory He had won.

> *Our salvation is no longer just a promise. It became a reality. His resurrection and ascension to God's throne proclaim the victory He had won.*

The moon shines by reflected light. To Adam, Abraham, and their descendants were given promises of a coming Redeemer. They were to sacrifice lambs to the Lord. The Lord directed Moses to build a sanctuary for Him. Then He gave instruction for a system of sacrifices and a yearly round of ceremonies to be observed. The temple services were to keep the nation connected to God. They reflected light from the salvation which the Messiah would provide by His life, death, and resurrection. The earthly temple services have ended. That was evidenced by the rending of the temple veil when Christ died. The placing of the moon under her feet is pictured, hereby indicating that the earthly temple services are past. The sacrifices were fulfilled in Christ. The light of the sun is upon her. The Aaronic priesthood has been replaced by Christ and His ministry in heaven. "We have a new, a living way" to God and salvation. Because of Christ's victorious life and death, His bride is now clothed with the saving glory of "the Sun of righteousness" (Mal. 4:2; Luke 2:30, 32; 2 Cor. 3:3–11).

A Woman, Her Child and the Dragon (Revelation 12)

Satan did all he could to destroy Abraham's seed and prevent the promises of God from becoming a reality. The man-child was born, lived the life of victory, died in our behalf, and is now at the throne of God, mediating His salvation to whoever will repent and come in faith to Him as their Lord and Savior. Verse 10 tells us that when Jesus died, His rulership was secured. Revelation 19:15 tells when it will be enforced. Previous prophets had told of this (see Ps. 2:9; Isaiah. 11:1, 4).

Verses 6 and 14 depict how God's people of faith "fled to the wilderness." God preserved His gospel and people of faith. The prophetic period of time (vs. 6 and 14) was referred to twice in chapter 11. It is found once more in chapter 13. It is first referred to in Daniel's prophecies (7:25) as a "little horn" that grew great, spoke blasphemously against God, and persecuted his people for "a time, times, and half a time." Daniel 12:7 refers again to that period of time. John, (Rev. 12:14) uses the identical phrase, "time, times, and half a time," to refer to the length of time the woman was preserved in the wilderness. This indicates that Daniel 7 and Revelation 12 refer to the same event (In Daniel's day, "a time, times, and half a time" was the way to refer to that length of time. Six hundred years later, forty-two months or 1,260 days could be used just as well. As Daniel 12:10 states, "none of the wicked understand, but the wise shall understand." That time event has been fulfilled in Christian history.

Revelation.12:17—This end-time war of Satan against the "remnant of her seed" is presented in chapter 13. Satan builds upon that which he had accomplished through the four kingdoms of Daniel 7, and then through the blasphemous little horn power of Daniel 7 and 8 during the Middle Ages. The first beast of Revelation 13 clearly identifies with Daniel 7 and 8 in its actions and being "wounded." This beast/little horn power, upon recovering from its mortal wound, exerts great influence in our world. Satan deceives the second beast power to support the first beast in enforcing its false worship (see Rev. 13:11–17). This false worship constitutes the "third woe" (Rev.11:14). It brings the seven last plagues, resulting in the collapse of Babylon.

A Brief Outline of Satan's War Against Christ

Job 1:6 and 2:1 indicate that Satan had some access to heaven. He had been banished from his position, but his motives and character had not been fully seen by the angels (see Isa. 14:12–17; Ezek. 28:11–19). However, in his treatment of Jesus, he demonstrated fully the ruthlessness of his self-serving idolatry and "there was no longer a place found for" the dragon and his angels in heaven (Rev. 12:8).

Jesus' life demonstrated that God was not self-serving. He sacrificed Himself for the sake of those He had created. Any question about God's goodness that could be asked is, in Christ, answered in God's favor. "God is good and does good" (Ps. 119:68).

Any standing that Satan might have had among the host of heaven, he destroyed by his treatment of Christ. Satan knows that his days are limited (see Rev. 12:10–12).

Satan began a war against God in heaven and did not prevail. Satan won over Adam and Eve. He won most of the world before the flood, but God preserved a remnant. God brought the nation of Israel into existence to be His servant. Satan warred to keep Israel from accomplishing God's purpose. He corrupted the nation, but God always had His people of faith, His remnant.

Jesus, the promised seed, came through the line of Abraham, Isaac, and Jacob, the tribe of Judah and David. He was born in Bethlehem of Judah. In His humanity, He lived a life that defeated Satan and all of his claims. He said, "I have kept My Father's commandments." His, holy, righteous, and good life, demonstrated God's Law.

Satan carries on his war against the church which Christ is building (see vs.13–15). He did this by persecution and introducing false practices and teachings into Christianity. When Constantine recognized and supported Roman Christianity, a union of church and state began that would destroy the gospel of Christ. As the authority of church and state merged, whole groups of people embraced the official religion. They were not converted to Christ. They brought their former religious practices with them.

Revelation 13, Two Beasts and the Mark

The word "beast" is used often in the Bible. It usually refers to animals, but it is also used symbolically and prophetically for nations or governments (see Dan. 7:17, 23, 24; Rev. 17:10, 12).

The first animal specifically named in the Bible is the serpent. Sheep are the second named animal. "The dragon of old, the Serpent" and the Lamb are also the last two animals named in the Bible (see Gen. 3:1; 4:2; Rev. 20:2; 22:1, 3). They are the contestants in our world's story. People are disciples of one or the other.

The first beast of Revelation 13 looks like none ever seen on earth. It, like the four beasts of Daniel 7, rises up from the sea. That places it among the nations of Europe. It is a composite of them with added features. It, like Daniel's fourth kingdom and the little horn power, makes war against the saints. They do so for identical time periods (see Dan. 7:25; Rev. 13:5). The, "time, times, half a time", "forty-two months", and "1,260 days" (Dan. 7:25; 12:7; Rev. 11:2, 3; 12:6, 14; 13:5), used interchangeably, prophetically equal 1,260 years.

Its difference is that its power and control comes not from military might, but by its "speaking". It claims to speak as God and for God. People are deceived into believing that it speaks as God and for God. This is why kings and nations used their power to support it and destroy its enemies. It is also why it is identified as blaspheming God in both Daniel's and John's prophecies.

It received a "deadly wound", but was healed (Rev. 13:3). The ideas of the Enlightenment, the opening words of The Declaration of Independence, and success of the American Revolution spread the belief that government should be by and for the people, rather than by kings and popes. The French Revolution was a reaction to the abuses caused by the union of church and state. "Liberty and Equality" were its cry. It greatly added to the turmoil in Europe. In 1798, the pope of Rome was taken prisoner by a French General and exiled from Rome. Many thought that would end his position and power. However, in 1929, the pope, in a Treaty with Italy, was recognized and the Vatican State was restored to him. Since then the political and religious influence of the Papacy has greatly increased. This fits the description of Revelation 13:3.

Revelation 11:7 introduced "the beast from the abyss." Revelation 12:8 identifies it as Satan and his angels. They no longer have any place in heaven. Cast out into the darkness of space, Satan, by his temptation and defeat of Adam and Eve, was able to make this earth the headquarters of his work. He is the enemy of God. The beast from the abyss does not work as an independent power, but through earthly powers. He gave his power, throne, and authority to the beast (Rev. 13:2).

Remember, Revelation unmasks Satan's war against God and His people. It is not presenting a general world history. In His letters to the seven churches, Christ referred to Satan, his seat, synagogue, and deceptive work (see 2:9, 10, 13, 24; 3:9). It is Satan who is behind all these efforts to destroy the gospel and the church. He has used individuals, governments, and other organizations to accomplish his goal.

When Christ gave these messages to John and told him to write it in a book for the churches, Babylon, Persia, Greece no longer ruled. The fourth kingdom, Rome, ruled. The prophetic beast of Revelation 13:1–8 was in the future. It is a composite of the beasts of Daniel 7. Now we can look back at church history and locate it. The seven heads represent the earthly powers through which the dragon had worked, was then working, and would in the future work, in his war against Christ. More information about the seven-headed beast is given in chapter 17.

The activities of the beast of Revelation 13:1–8 parallel the activities of the little horn of Daniel. There is blasphemy against

Revelation 13, Two Beasts and the Mark

God. It wars against the saints. There is the identical prophetic period. Satan gives to this beast the power that he offered Christ when tempting Him. "The dragon gave him his power, seat, and great authority." The city of Rome became the capitol of a great religious empire. Titles and honors emperors had used were claimed by its bishop. One head is wounded, but then it is healed (vs. 2–4). This event adds to the wonder and honor which the world gives to this power. By its speaking "great things in blasphemies against God" and its manner of working, the beast persecutes the woman—God's people—as pictured in Revelation 12:9, 13–17.

Revelation 13:11–18 presents another beast with different characteristics. It does not arise out of the sea. It is located in a part of the earth that is different from where the previous beasts were located. It rises to power following the deadly wound of the first beast. It does not war against or replace the first beast. It gives all its support to the blasphemous claims and worship of the first beast. It has two "lamb-like horns." Twenty-eight times in Revelation, the word "lamb" is used to refer to Christ. This one use here indicates that the nation is identified as Christian. The United States was founded on the idea of "freedom and justice for all." Political and religious freedoms are supported by its Constitution. With these freedoms, and as a haven for oppressed people, it has been "lamb-like".

The nation changes. In contrast from appearing "lamb-like", it will speak as a dragon, with the same authority with which the first beast speaks. As a superpower, it will support the first beast. It will be enabled to perform great signs by which it convinces the world to make an image to the first beast and worship it. Eventually it is able to get the death sentence invoked against anyone who will not do so. Revelation calls it "the false prophet" (16:13; 19:20; 20:10).

6 6 6

This is "the number of the beast, the number found in his name." Each pope takes a different name, but his claim remains the same. He is "Vicar of the Son of God." Latin was the official language used by the Roman Church until after the middle of the 20th century. The numerical value of the letters in the Latin title, Vicarius Filii Dei, add up to 666. The Greek letters in *Lateninos* ("Latin-speaking man"), *He Latine Basileia* ("The Latin Kingdom"), and *Italika Ekklesia* ("Italian Church") each add up to 666. "The number of his name is 666" (R.A. Anderson, *Unfolding The Revelation*, pp. 131–134).

The seven heads of the beast of Revelation 13 and 17 are not named. History, as unfolded in the prophecies of Daniel 2, 7, 8, and 9, gives some understanding (Rev. 17 adds more).

C. Mervyn Maxwell identifies the seven heads of Rev. 17 as follows: The five that are fallen are Babylon, Media-Persia, Greece, Rome, and Papal Rome. The sixth is "the one that is not." The power of the papacy was broken when civil government took the pope prisoner. However, passing time has restored him to greater respect and influence than before. The seventh is the uniting of the beast, dragon, and false prophet to enforce religious practice (see *God Cares,* vol. 2, pp. 474–478). Some see the "eighth" as a time in which Satan impersonates Christ.

Satan's war against the remnant (12:17) reaches its climax in the enforcement of the mark of the beast (13:11–18). Christ wars against the false speaking of the two beast powers "with the sword of His mouth" (Rev. 2:16). God's Word, as given in the Bible, is always the defense and strength of His people.

The Mark of the Beast

Bring up the subject of Bible prophecy and people ask, "What about the mark of the beast?" The mark of the beast is much more than a curious topic of conversation. When the events of Revelation 13:12–17 occur, every living person will have to make a choice. The most solemn warnings in all the Bible warn against receiving the mark. The seven last plagues are sent upon those who have the mark of the beast (see Rev. 14:9–11; 16:2; 19:20)

Everyone gets the mark of the beast, right? No. Revelation takes notice of Christ's people of faith who get the victory over the beast and his mark.

What is the mark? The mark is not 666; that's "the number of his name." Is it a plastic identification that brings about our bondage to world financial powers? No; that's called a credit card. Is it a literal tattoo in the flesh of our forehead and hand? No; that's only found in the book of Hollywood and novels about the end-time, not in Bible prophecy.

How do we identify the beast and his mark? How do we avoid receiving the mark? John wrote that God wants us to understand and keep these things.

Sitting at the piano and playing beautiful music is a mystery to some, but not to those who have learned to read music and interpret all of that through their fingers and onto the keyboard. In like manner, understanding Revelation depends on learning not too difficult rules of interpretation.

"No prophecy is to be privately interpreted. The prophecy did not come by human choice but holy men spoke (wrote) as they were moved by the Holy Spirit" (2 Peter 1:20, 21). With our mind open to God's will and praying for the Holy Spirit to give us understanding, we can discover God's truth.

The Mark of the Beast

Where is it presented? It is first mentioned in Revelation 13:16–17. It is mentioned six more times in the book of Revelation. God warns us not to receive it. There are terrible results for those who do (see Rev. 14:9–11; 16:2; 19:20, 21). There are rewards for those who get the victory over the beast, his image, and mark (see Rev. 15:2; 20:4).

What are the beasts? According to Daniel 7:17 and other Bible passages, a beast represents a nation or sovereign, governing power. The mark of the beast does not stand alone. What is its cause? The mark of the beast has to do with worship (see Rev. 13:12, 15). In each of the above warning texts, it is connected with worship. It is a false worship taught by the first beast and supported and enforced by the second. It is worship that serves as the sign of loyalty to the beast power. The mark of the beast is worship imposed by the power of government (see 13:14–17; 14:6–12). This worship is in conflict with God's law and the message to "fear God and give glory to Him for the hour of His judgment is come and worship him who created all things".

How is it Possible That People Will Do This (Rev. 13:13, 14; 19:20)?

By the signs and miracles performed, people are led to accept the false teaching. When Jesus answered the question of His disciples regarding the destruction of Jerusalem and the end time (Matthew 24:2, 3), He said that false christs and prophets would appear doing great signs and wonders that would, if possible, deceive the elect (see Matt. 24:23–27: also 2 Thess. 2:3–12).

How does the prophecy identify those who remain faithful to God? "Here are those who keep the commandments of God and the faith of Jesus" (Rev. 12:17; 14:12). The mark of the beast involves worship. It will occur when the nations of Europe, North America, and South America unite in enforcing a religious practice that conflicts with God's law. It will be Sunday observance in place of God's seventh-day Sabbath.

This may be thought of as impossible, but since the United States was founded, there has been continuous effort to give legal standing to Sunday. Formerly, it was to recognize Sunday as the Christian Sabbath. Now it is being presented as a needed benefit for workers and family solidarity. It will come. Revelation is not about earthly politics. It deals with politics only when earthly events impact Christ's gospel and church.

(See, Mark of the Beast–2, in the Appendix).

Revelation 14

Revelation 14 begins with the Lamb standing on Mount Zion, and with Him are 144,000 redeemed people. Here again is pictured the assurance that though death threats have been made by the beast and his image, God will have a faithful, victorious remnant. The 144,000 were first introduced in chapter 7. It is said that they are servants of God and the winds of strife and disaster would be held until they were sealed in their foreheads. Here the sealing has occurred; they have the Father's name written on their foreheads.

Revelation 7:4 reads, "I heard the number of those who were sealed. One hundred and forty-four thousand of all the tribes of the children of Israel were sealed." It then says that there were to be 12,000 from each of the tribes. The list of tribes omits the tribe of Dan. Joseph and his son Manasseh are included in the list, but not Joseph's other son, Ephraim. When John looked to see, he did not see twelve tribes. What he saw was a great multitude which no man could number of all nations, tribes, and people standing before the throne and the Lamb. Jews and people from all nations will be among the redeemed. "They came out of the great tribulation" (v. 14). That white-robed throng includes those referred to in Revelation 6:10,11, who also suffered the same as those who go through the final great tribulation.

In light of the brief mention of the 144,000 in chapters 7 and 14, it is best to say that the 144,000 is a symbolic number. It is composed of twelve 12,000s. Twelve is said to be God's kingdom number, a representation of His people. Numbering in the Bible did not include woman and children. Many women and children were martyred and will be among the saved. The twelve gates of the New Jerusalem have the names of the twelve tribes of the children of Israel written on them. All who enter the city do so as God's Israel. On the twelve foundations of the city are written the names of the twelve apostles. The apostles were the ones God used to establish His church, which is His true Israel on earth.

Revelation's list is different from the two lists given in Ezekiel 48. In this passage, the list for the portions of the tribes omit Joseph but name both his sons, making thirteen. The list for the gates is limited to the twelve sons of Jacob.

(To know more about Israel, see, "MESSIAH AND THE ISRAEL OF GOD, in the Appendix).

The 144,000 are described as "not defiled with women, for they are virgins." (Rev. 14:4) This is to be understood with verse 8. Babylon makes all nations drink of her fornication, but the 144,000 refuse to accept any teaching and worship that is contrary to God's Word. They are the remnant of the pure woman of Revelation 12, against whom the dragon wars. It is the three-fold message of Revelation 14:6–12 that has been their proclamation and defense.

"Another angel, the second one, followed, saying, 'Fallen, fallen is Babylon the great, she who has made all nations drink of the wine of the passion of her immorality'" (14:8). This is the first mention of Babylon in the book of Revelation. It tells us judgment is passed on Babylon. Babylon stands in opposition to the woman of Revelation 12, against whom Satan wars. All nations have embraced Babylon's ways. The teachings of Babylon conflict with the gospel and all of God's Word.

The name "Babylon" occurs five more times in Revelation (16:19; 17:5; 18:2, 10, 21). She is also referred to as "that great city" and "harlot" (17:1, 5, 15, 16, 18; 18:10, 16, 18, 19, 21). Other references to Babylon in the NT are Matthew 1:11, 12, 17 and Acts 7:43. These references speak of the "carrying away into Babylon." That event was significant to the Jews. It stood as a pivotal date in their history. They had not been an independent nation since that happened. That the word "Babylon" had symbolic meaning for Jews is evident by Peter's use of the name (1 Peter 5:13), for Babylon, as a city, did not exist any longer. "It is known that early Christians used the cryptic title, 'Babylon,' when speaking

Revelation 14

of Rome to avoid political reprisals" (SDA Bible Commentary, vol. 7, p. 589; *also see* p. 830).

The message of the third angel provides more understanding of what the angels are telling us. The language refers us back to Revelation 13—the worship and mark of the beast. Those who refuse to heed the call of the first angel and continue imbibing the teaching (wine) of Babylon will receive God's judgment of destruction (14:17–19). Christ gave us Revelation so that we would know these things and not be deceived by Babylon. As He ends Revelation, He says, "I Jesus have sent my angel to testify to you these things for the churches" (22:16). The entire book is for the churches.

In the messages to the seven churches (chapters 2 and 3), warning was given of false teachers and teachings that were coming into Christianity. History reveals that there were Christians who heard "what the Spirit said to the churches" and remained true to Christ. However, many accommodated the falsehoods and "a falling away" (2 Thess. 2:3–5) came into Christianity. When Emperor Constantine united Roman Christianity to his government, false teachings—the "wine of Babylon"—began to take over Christianity.

Revelation 12 reveals who is behind the efforts to destroy God's gospel and church. Satan began his war against God in heaven. He had worked to destroy the faith given to Israel and prevent the promised Messiah. He warred against Christ from His birth. He worked to destroy the woman—Christ's Church. His final war is against the "remnant who keep the commandments of God and hold to the testimony of Jesus" (12:17).

The message of the third angel reveals that Satan's war against the remnant climaxes in governments enforcing the worship of the beast and its image—receiving the mark of the beast (see 13:11–18).

What the Three Angels of Revelation 14 Tell Us

The first messenger (vs. 6, 7) is flying through the heavens. His message is to go all around the earth, "to every nation, tribe, language and people." All the world is to hear it. This reinforces Matthew 24:14 and 28:19. He does not have his feet on the land and sea as does the angel in Revelation 10. He moves through the sky. The description somewhat fits modern life. Today we travel and communicate through the heavens, just as the angel is pictured.

What is the message of the first angel? His message emphasizes three truths. The first is the "eternal gospel." The gospel is God's solution for all the ills of humanity. The birth, life, death, and resurrection of Jesus constitute the greatest news of all. The gospel of our Lord Jesus Christ is as vital today as it has ever been. The destiny of earth and all its people are determined by Him. Thus, it behooves us to "Fear God"—acknowledge and reverence Him—"give Him glory"—live a life that reflects His goodness—and "worship Him" as the Creator.

Our world loves to give glory to mankind, for humans have accomplished much. Technology has made life very comfortable. Medicine has done much to relieve illness. Promises are made that cancer, AIDS, and all the rest will be conquered. Consider our military power. Who can stand against us? We tend to be self-absorbed, and God is given no place, no glory, though our lives come from Him

We must admit that our technology is powerless to supply the world's greatest need, which is to become the people we were intended to be. God does this through the gospel. The message, "Fear God, give glory to Him", calls people to repentance and a new life. The gospel changes people. They are empowered to live lives that honor God and embody the "golden rule" (see Matt. 7:12). God is to be recognized and worshipped as our Creator. God's creatorship is basic to all that He claims. If He is not our Creator, He can have no claim on us except by enslaving us. If we came into existence without Him, why would we need Him? We would continue without Him.

God's fourth commandment, "keep holy the Sabbath day," tells us how we honor and give Him worship as the Creator. This fits with Revelation 12:17 and 14:12. God's "remnant", the "saints", keep God's commandments. The reason for this message is because "the hour of His judgment has come." Revelation 10–14 tells us that the gospel has come to its climax. It ends with the harvest of the earth. Jesus spoke of this in the parables of Matthew 13, His instruction in Matthew 24, and here in Revelation 14:14–19 and chapter 19. The annual Jewish Day of Atonement prefigured judgment day. God's judgment is visualized in Daniel 7 and mentioned throughout the Bible. "As in the days of Noah," the message of God's judgment is given to the earth.

Babylon in the Book of Revelation. Revelation 14:8

When the New Testament was written, the old city of Babylon was in ruins. Jeremiah's prophecy that she would fall and not be rebuilt had come to pass (see Jer. 51:3–7, 59–64). The second of the heavenly messengers of Revelation 14 names her. "Fallen, fallen is Babylon the great, she who has made all nations drink of the wine of the wrath of her immorality." The name "Babylon" occurs five more times in Revelation (16:19; 17:5; 18:2, 10). She is also referred to as "that great city" and "harlot" (17:1, 2, 18; 18:16, 18, 19, 21).

That the word "Babylon" had come to have a symbolic meaning is evident by Peter's use of the name (1 Peter 5:13), for Babylon as a city did not then exist. In Revelation 17:5, the designation "mystery Babylon" specifically identifies the name as figurative or symbolic, just as in 1 Peter 5:13. "It is known that early Christians used the cryptic title, 'Babylon,' when speaking of Rome to avoid political reprisals" (*Seventh-day Adventist Bible Commentary*, vol. 7, pp. 589, 830).

As with many other words and expressions in the book, the significance of Babylon in Revelation is best understood in terms of its counterpart in the Old Testament. Historically, prophetically, and literally, Babylon stands as the rival to God and His truth. Babylon is an earthly organization claiming to rule for God.

Following the destruction of the earth by the flood, Babel is the first city mentioned. There the people of earth united to build a tower that would "reach to heaven" (Gen. 10:10; 11:1–9). The Babylonians regarded the tower as "the house of the foundation of heaven and earth" (*International Standard Bible Encyclopedia*, vol. 1, p. 357).

Babylon is not anti-religious. Babylon is very religious. "Because Babylon contained the sanctuary of the god Marduke, considered to be the Lord of heaven and earth, the chief of all the gods, the ancient Babylonians considered their city the 'navel' of the world. Babylon was a religious center without a rival on earth. A cuneiform tablet of Nebuchadnezzar's time lists 53 temples dedicated to important gods, 955 small sanctuaries, and 384 street altars, all of them within the cities confines" (*Seventh-day Adventist Bible Commentary*, vol. 4, p. 797).

For Babylonians, "Babel" meant "Gate of God" or "Gate of the Gods", for Babylon was the place where the gods consorted with men to order the affairs of earth. The people were to look to Babylon to know God's will.

> *Babylon is not anti-religious. Babylon is very religious.*

The Assyrian King List contains the notation for various kings that "the king took the hand of Bel. That is, the king went through the New Year's Coronation Ceremony at Babylon. This ceremony was the rite of receiving the kingship from the God Bel. All Babylonian kings did this annually" (*Seventh-day Adventist Bible Commentary*, vol. 2, p. 157).

Cyrus, the Persian ruler, in writing of his conquest of Babylon, wrote, "Marduke, the great lord warmed the hearts of the Babylonians towards me. I am Cyrus, king of all, The great king, the mighty king, king of Babylon, king of Sumer and Akkad, king of the four corners of the earth." (R.A. Anderson, *Unfolding Daniel's Prophecies*, pp. 81, 82).

Is there any person today who claims God has bestowed upon him authority over all the earth?

Revelation's Babylon has been very active, for the angel states that judgment has been passed on her. Babylon is "she". She stands in opposition to the woman of Revelation 12, against whom Satan makes war. Old Babylon took the vessels of God's temple and used them to magnify her ways and teachings (see Dan. 5). Last-

Babylon in the Book of Revelation. Revelation 14:8

day Babylon does the same. All nations have embraced Babylon's ways. The teachings of Babylon conflict with the gospel and the teachings of the Bible.

Other references to Babylon in the New Testament are Matthew 1:11, 12, 17 and Acts 7:43. These references speak of "the carrying away into Babylon." That event was significant to the Jews. They had not been an independent nation since it happened. Babylon stood as the rival and destroyer of "the people of God."

Babylon was sometimes considered the "navel" or "center" of the world because it was from Babel that the people went out and settled all over the earth. Babylon was referred to as "Mother." The Hebrew regarded Jerusalem as "Mother" and God's center for the world. They associated the name Babel or Babylon with *halal*, a word meaning "to confuse" (see Gen. 11:9).

The founders of Babylon, in great self-confidence, proposed their dream: "A tower to reach to heaven." Probably not literally, but "here we will bring God down to instruct us." The tower builders devised a human plan to connect God to their world, ignoring the fact that from the beginning God had been communicating with His world.

Deuteronomy 30:12 condemns the idea that humans must do things to cause God to come to them. He has spoken in various ways. He has revealed Himself in nature, His Word, and Jesus Christ. He has issued His invitation: "Whoever will may come!"

Rome Replaced Babylon

The Babylon of Revelation sits on seven mountains or hills. This fits Rome, not ancient Babylon (17:9; the Greek word *oros* is translated both as "hill" and "mountain"). Revelation 2:12–13 refers to Pergamos, not to Rome, as the place of Satan's seat or throne. R.A. Anderson, in his book *Unfolding The Revelation*, traces the steps by which Babylonian religion settled in Rome. "When Persia conquered Babylon the inhabitants of the city were given their freedom. The Babylonian priests later led a revolt and were driven from the city. 'The defeated Chaldeans fled to Asia Minor and fixed their central college at Pergamos, and took the Palladium of Babylon, the cubic stone, with them. Here independent of State control they carried on the rites of their religion' (Wm. B. Barker, *Lares and Penates*. pp. 232, 233). Pergamos became the 'seat' (Rev. 2:13) of the satanic system of Babylonian mysteries" (p. 23).

"Pergamos was for some time the headquarters of this mystery cult. But when the king of Pergamos bequeathed his kingdom to the Romans, this whole cult was transferred to Rome, which since has been the headquarters of this false system" (p. 24).

In 29 B.C., Emperor Augustus had a temple dedicated to himself and built in Pergamos. This marked the beginning of emperor worship in the Roman provinces. He assumed the title "Pontific Maximus," which meant "chief high priest" of the empire. This title, the "keys", and the vestments were all taken over by apostate Christianity (pp. 24, 25; *Seventh-day Adventist Bible Commentary*, vol. 7. pp. 73, 91; vol. 9, p. 1178).

Ancient, Literal Babylon

"You who dwell by many waters" (Jer. 51:13) "A golden cup in the Lord's hand" (Jer. 51:7).

"Babylon is fallen" (Isa. 21:9; Jer. 51:8). "I shall be a mistress forever...I shall not sit as a widow" (Jer. 47:7, 8).

"Go out of the midst of her my people" Jer. 51:45 "At her fall the heavens and the earth...shall sing for joy." Jer. 51:48 "As a stone shall Babylon sink and Rise no more." (Jer. 51:64).

Symbolic Babylon

"Seated on many waters" (Rev. 17:1). "Holds a golden cup" (Rev. 17:4).

"Fallen, fallen is Babylon" (Rev. 14:8; 18:2). "A queen I sit, I am no widow" (Rev. 18:7).

"Come out of her my people" (Rev. 18:4). At her fall, "heaven, saints, apostles and prophets rejoice" (Rev. 18:20). "Like a great millstone thrown into the sea Babylon shall be thrown down" (Rev. 18:21).

Two Cities are Presented in Revelation

The New Jerusalem: 3:12; 21:2; 21:10

The holy city Jerusalem: 21:2; 21:10; the holy city: 21:14–16, 18, 19, 21, 23; 22:14, 19

Babylon, the great city: 18:10, 16, 18, 19, 21

Babylon in the Book of Revelation. Revelation 14:8

Two Women are Represented in Revelation

(1) "The woman clothed with the sun": 12:1
(2) Babylon, the great harlot and the mother of harlots: 17:1, 5

The dragon, Satan, attempted to destroy the promised child of the sun-clothed woman (Rev. 12:4, 5). He persecuted the woman (v. 13) and attempted to drown her by flooding Christianity with people who held to his deceptions (vs. 9, 15). This woman survived in the wilderness for 1,260 prophetic days (v. 6). Then the earth opened up and enabled the woman to survive (v. 16). She is the "Bride, the Lamb's wife" (Rev. 19:7, 8; 21:2, 9, 10).

New Jerusalem is referred to as both city and people. It is people, God's people, that fill her with life. It is for people that Christ came into this world. This world was created to be inhabited. All is restored through Christ.

The woman, Babylon the great, the mother of harlots, is how Revelation 17 describes her. Like Queen Jezebel, who is referred to in Revelation 2:20, Babylon gets what she wants because "people, multitudes, nations, and languages" (v. 15) have been taught that she represents God. She is also referred to as a city (see v. 18).

Armageddon

"Doomsday" for civilization is how movies and books have presented Armageddon. In the last century, there have appeared among Christians many changing ideas about Armageddon. It has been viewed as political warfare centered in Palestine with modern Israel, oil reserves, and anti-Christians involved. Previously, the Communistic Soviet Union was the villain. Now China and Islam are suggested. Whatever the current political situation is, it is made to fit into the scenario.

Here are two definitions for "Armageddon": *World Book Encyclopedia*—"The place where the rulers of the world will fight the last great battle between good and evil." *Webster's New College Dictionary*—"Bible. The place where the final, decisive battle between the forces of good and evil is to be fought before Judgment Day. Rev. 16:16." What does the Bible say about Armageddon (see Rev. 16:13–16)?

It appears that the word originated with John's writing. As a Hebrew word, it is a combination of two words: *Har* = "mount" and *mageddon* = "Megiddo"—Mount Megiddo. What is perplexing is that no such mountain is known. Megiddo was a fortress city that controlled the whole plain of Esdraelon (Mt. Carmel bordered the northwestern end of that plain). Zechariah 12:11 and 2 Chronicles 35:22 refer to war and mourning on the plain of Megiddo.

"As no Mount Megiddo is known to either ancient or modern geographers, it appears more likely that in a book abounding in symbolical language this term (Mount Megiddo) also should be meant to carry a symbolic meaning...It is to be noted moreover, that the battle said to take place on this spot is clearly one of ideologies, (the gospel versus the 'bad spell.') God's truth opposed to Satan's error" (*Interpreter's Dictionary of the Bible*, vol. I, p. 227). Prominent biblical examples of such ideological warfare are Elijah's contest with the prophets of Baal on adjacent Mt. Carmel and Babylon's enforced worship of Nebuchadnezzar's great image, recorded in Daniel 3.

There is more we can learn about the battle of Armageddon from Revelation. The word "battle" in Rev. 16:14 (KJV) is translated from the Greek word *polemos*. *Polemos* occurs fifteen times in Revelation. In the KJV, it is translated eight times as "war", four times as "battle", and three times as "fight". "The Greek has at least two words to indicate hostilities: *polemos*, meaning "war", and *mache*, meaning "battle". Archbishop Trench, in *Synonyms of the New Testament*, p. 322, remarks: "Polemos and Mache often occur together...there is the same difference between them as between our own, war, and, battle... The Peloponnesian War... the Battle of Marathon... polemos, embraces the whole course of hostilities -war; mache, the actual shock in arms of hostile armies." W.E. Reed, Review and Herald, March 18, 1954

Whenever the Greek word *polemos* occurs in the prophecies of Revelation, it is the conflict between God's truth and Satan's errors that is the issue. Revelation is not making predictions about earthly military contests.

Keep in mind the two main themes of Revelation. They are:

The revealing of the victorious Christ who, by His life and death on earth, vindicated God and solved the problem of sin. All the promises and symbols of redemption became a reality in Him. He, the All-Sufficient One, is fully involved with His church. He leads her from triumph to triumph.

Christ's warfare on earth is always done "in righteousness." Revelation unmasks the efforts of Satan to destroy the gospel and church—God's truth and people. Unable to destroy Christ's church, he seeks to take over Christianity and use it for his purposes.

These two themes are evident as we consider the warfare that is portrayed in the book of Revelation. There is a war waged by the Lord. "Repent, or else I am coming to you quickly and will war against them with the sword of My mouth"—those who hold the doctrine of Balaam or the Nicolaitans (Rev. 2:16).

Armageddon

Michael and His angels fought against the dragon (12:7). The Lamb overcomes the beast and the ten horn powers that make war against Him (17:14; 19:14). In righteousness, He judges and makes war. From the beginning, it has been "in righteousness" that God has waged His war.

There is a war waged by Satan (the dragon) and his followers: 9:7, 9 — He utilized Islam's conquest of many areas where Christianity had been established and its denial of Christ as Son of God.

11:17—The beast from the abyss wars against God's two witnesses in The French Revolution. The union of the church and government had become so oppressive and unfair that to achieve freedom, religion was outlawed. The same situation fueled the Russian rejection of religion (The "enlightenment" developed into atheism, naturalism, and the theory of evolution, which war against God's two witnesses, the Old and New Testaments).

12:4, 7—There was war in heaven against Michael and His angels. Satan and his angels were thrown down to earth where he continues his war against the Man-child—Christ.

12:13, 14—Satan's 1,260-year war against the woman (God's church hid in the wilderness).

12:17—Satan's final war against the remnant who keep the commandments of God and hold to the testimony of Jesus.

Satan's war against the remnant is revealed in Revelation 13:12–17. His last strategy is to impose severe penalties for those who refuse to follow the worship imposed by the beast and his image. The worship of the beast and his image becomes the issue in the remainder of the prophecies of Revelation. "Who is like the beast? Who is able to wage war with him (13:4)?" The world is deceived (see vs. 6, 7). The beast continues the war against God and His truth. He blasphemes God, His name, and temple and makes war against His saints on earth (his activities identify him with Daniel 7:21–25; 8:10, 11, 24; Matt. 24:21, 22; 2 Thess. 2:3, 4).

The new, second beast of Revelation 13 does not replace the first beast as did the beasts of Daniel 7 and 8. Lamb-likeness in its founding principles, but it changes. It becomes a world power and uses its authority to support the beast. It is referred to as "the false prophet" (16:13; 19:20; 20:10).

Armageddon's Glorious End

From the dragon, beast, and false prophet, the spirits of devils go to the rulers of the earth and the whole world to gather them for the war of the great day of God the Almighty (see 16:13, 14). Their success is seen in 17:14 and 19:19. "The beast and ten horn powers make war with the Lamb." "The beast and the rulers of earth and their armies are gathered together to make war against Christ and His army."

Revelation 17:15–18 reveals the results of the "drying up of the Euphrates" (sixth plague). The dragon's confederacy falls apart. They realize that they have been deceived.

Revelation 19 presents the climax of the gospel when Christ comes in power and glory. God's true people of faith, the bride of the Lamb, have kept faithful. The beast and false prophet are thrown into the lake of fire. The rest are killed with the "sword which came out of the mouth of Him who sat upon the white horse" (vs. 20, 21). Christ's deliverance of His faithful people is as dramatic as was the deliverance of Israel at the Red Sea.

Christ's deliverance of His faithful people is as dramatic as was the deliverance of Israel at the Red Sea.

It becomes evident that the war of Armageddon is not a political war between earthly governments. It is an event with similarities to Elijah's conflict with the prophets of Baal on Mount Carmel (see 1 Kings 18) and the contest involving the great image which Nebuchadnezzar set up on the Plain of Dura (Dan. 3). It is seen in the Reformation, in the question, "Where does a person look for salvation." Is it to Christ, His Word, and ministry for us at the throne of God, or is it to the church with its teaching regarding its sacraments and priesthood? In Revelation, it climaxes over an enforced worship which conflicts with God's law. As the war of the great day of God, it ends the great rebellion against God that began in heaven and, through the failure of Adam and Eve, was transferred to our world.

An important difference with Elijah's contest with the prophets of Baal is that then, "fire from heaven" was what indicated God's

Armageddon

side. Revelation 13:13 tells us that in Satan's final deception, he "makes fire come down from heaven in the sight of men." This means that God's people will have to overcome as did Christ in His wilderness temptation. He worked no miracle. He quoted God's Word from Scripture, the sword of God. That is what Adam and Eve should have done in Eden. Those who overcome stay with God's Word as He has given it in the Bible. They do not allow Satan's appealing deceptions to find a home in their thinking. They refuse to obey the beast's law and continue their obedience to God's law. "They overcome by the blood of the Lamb and the word of their testimony" (Rev. 12:11). If we focus on the Christ of Revelation rather than on the beast, we will be found on Christ's side when He ends Armageddon.

Seven Last Plagues (Revelation 15 and 16)

Chapter 14 ends by picturing two harvests. Verses 14–16 picture God's harvest when Christ comes to earth for His people as He described it in Matthew 24:30–31.

The other harvest (vs. 17–20) is of those who worshiped the beast. They refused Christ's heaven-sent messages. For the two groups to be identified, a heavenly judgment had to have occurred. That judgment was announced by the first of the three angels.

Before describing the plagues, the vision pictures those who were victorious over the beast. In their song of Moses and the Lamb, they sing of the majesty of God and that His judgments are true and righteous. This is given to encourage us. Christ does not want the threats and persecutions from the world to cause His followers to give up. This same type of encouragement is given in 7:4–17 and in 14:1–5. The fact that the saved are a great multitude, more than can be numbered, is encouraging. It makes people believe 'I can be one of them.' 'I will sing the song of Moses and the Lamb.'

Romans 8:18 is true: "The sufferings of this present world are not worth being compared to the glory that shall be revealed in us." As terrible as the plagues are, they will be as nothing in the glorious eternity God provides for His people.

Revelation 15:6–8 remind us of how important Christ's ministry in heaven's temple is in the plan of salvation. Heaven's temple is the control center of bringing the gospel to its climax. Christ's intercession, symbolized by the burning incense on the golden altar, is what gives guidance and protection to His people. His intercession becomes more intense as the pre-Advent judgment in heaven is closing. When it ends, "no one was able to enter the temple." The day of salvation has passed. The words of Revelation 22:11—12 are pronounced.

Today we can still come "boldly to the throne of grace" for salvation and the help we need to live for Him. Faith can enter within the veil where Jesus our forerunner and High Priest ministers for us (Heb. 4:16; 6:18–20). When the plagues come, it is too late. God's Spirit has been grieved away. Revelation 16:9–11 states that the plagues do not cause any one to repent. God's righteous judgments increase their hatred of God and His people.

As global troubles increase and the plagues come, those who refuse the mark of the beast are threatened with death. They must live only by "the faith of Jesus." That means their decisions are based on God's Word. They keep the commandments of God, not the command of the beast. They trust the promises of God as given in the Bible.

The plagues are not universal. The first one is poured on the earth, the area of the second beast of Revelation 13. It had been foremost in making the image to the beast. Horrible-looking and painful sores appear on those who have the mark of the beast. The second plague falls on the sea. Every living creature in the sea dies. The third is on rivers and springs of water (see 16:4–7). Imagine the disaster that will bring. Psalm 91 will become very real and precious to God's faithful remnant.

The fourth plague results in intense global warming. It will feel as if the fires of hell have begun on earth. Imagine New York City reaching 130 degrees for a week. The fifth plague falls on the throne of the beast. Its kingdom is filled with darkness and despair. They had been promised and expected great and good results for the world. The plagues make them realize they are under God's judgment. Their disappointment leads to the collapse of Babylon, which occurs under the sixth plague (see 16:12–16).

The "drying up of the great River Euphrates" is the way the sixth plague is described. Ancient Babylon was nourished by the Euphrates River, which ran under its wall and through the city.

Seven Last Plagues (Revelation 15 and 16)

The water supply for the city was assured. Crops could be grown within its walls. Without the supporting water, the city would fall. The besieging army diverted the water of the river, so it no longer ran through the city. It "dried up." The Medo-Persian forces were able to walk under the wall into the city. They found that the gate from the city to the river had been left open. Like a thief, they entered Babylon (see Dan. 5:30, 31). Also notice Christ's words in Revelation 16:15. His coming "as a thief" follows the plagues.

Revelation's Babylon receives the support of all nations. The support was brought about by demonic-supplied miracles. The plagues make the nations realize they have been deceived. They turn against their harlot leadership. This leads to the collapse of the confederacy of the beast, dragon, and false prophet. It is further described in Revelation 17:12–17. The powers that make up Babylon turn on each other. Their goal to build the city of God on earth ends in disaster.

Under the seventh plague (Rev. 16:17–21), "a great-loud voice comes out of the temple in heaven from the throne." It is God's voice. It is not a strange voice. Its quiet pleading has often been heard and refused. Three words will be heard: "It is done."

The vibrations of this proclamation reach to the farthest point of God's universe. Babylon collapses. She is "done." The war of Armageddon is "done." Noises, lightning, and thunder accompany all this. The greatest earthquake of all time occurs. Islands disappear and mountains sink. All coastal regions are submerged by tremendous tsunamis. Imagine the terrible weather conditions necessary to produce the seventy-five-pound hail stones which bombard the earth (Job 38:22–23 predicted it). Stoning was the punishment prescribed by the Lord (Leviticus 20:2, 27; 24:11–14, 23) and is what He will use. No building or work of human hands is left. There is nothing left except for the coming of Christ. Chapters 17 and 18 give more information about God's final appeal, who composes Babylon, and its destruction.

Babylon Judged (Revelation 17 and 18)

Chapter 17 continues the vision of chapter 16. One of the plague angels says to John, "Come, I will show you the judgment of the great harlot who sits on many waters." This woman claims to be the bride of Christ–His church. She has become unfaithful to Him. She became a harlot by being more concerned about having the support of earthly rulers and nations than faithfully representing Christ and His saving gospel.

This corresponds to Christ's reproof to the Pergamos Church about Balaam. Balaam was called to be a prophet of the Lord. A foreign king heard of Balaam and offered him wealth if he would curse the Hebrew people. The Lord did not allow Balaam to do so. Balaam then advised the king to lead the people into fornication, and thus they would bring the curse of the law upon themselves. He used his prophetic leadership to acquire honor and riches for himself.

Jesus warned against this temptation in His parable of Matthew 21:33–41. When the owner of the vineyard sent his son to his vineyard, the caretakers of the vineyard killed him and took over the vineyard for their benefit. This is what the harlot woman has done. She has taken over Christianity as her kingdom. Verse 15 states that the "many waters where the harlot sits, are peoples, multitudes, nations and languages" that support her. Last-day Babylon is more than the Papacy. It is a confederacy that includes "the dragon, the beast, and the false prophet" (Rev. 16:13, 19; 7:12, 13, 15, 17). Babylon's leadership comes from the influence exerted by little Vatican City. "All the world marveled and followed the beast" (Rev. 13:3, NKJV). *

Christ, in giving this book for John to write and send to the churches, emphasizes the great issues of life. Those issues are: What is my origin? From where did I come? Why am I here? Is there any purpose for living? What is my destiny? Is there anything beyond our present existence?

Revelation 18 gives another vision. Verses 1–5 again reveal God's longsuffering efforts to bring people to salvation. A mighty messenger is sent from heaven. He adds great power to the appeal of the three angels of Revelation 14: "Babylon is fallen, is fallen, come out of her my people!" "You can escape her plagues. You will escape her plagues if you will only come out. The rest of chapter 18 describes the destruction of Babylon. It is presented in economic terms. That is because it is the global economy, not moral goodness, that causes the people of earth to work together. Self-serving is at the root of all of Babylon's efforts.

"Torment and sorrow" and "death, mourning, famine and burning," is how Revelation 18:7–8 describe her plagues. It is global economy — world business — that unites nations to act together. Verses 11–19 describe the collapse of all business. It results in the greatest depression the world has ever experienced. Babylon had used business, "no buying or selling," to force acceptance of the mark of the beast. The world economic collapse causes Babylon to endure the same punishment she prescribed. Babylon's war against God, His gospel, and church results in its destruction.

Christ, in giving this book for John to write and send to the churches, emphasizes the great issues of life. Those issues are: What is my origin? From where did I come? Why am I here? Is

Babylon Judged (Revelation 17 and 18)

there any purpose for living? What is my destiny? Is there anything beyond our present existence?

Revelation declares the glorious future God has for those who put their faith in Him. No wonder Satan has led people to set it aside as having no meaning for Christians today. They remain in darkness. Those who refuse the Bible and its worldview are unprepared for earth's final events. Christ's return to earth for His people will come to them "suddenly, like a thief" that confronts a person. They will not escape. How long do the plagues last? We are not given a particular time. Revelation 18:8 says Babylon's plagues come in one day. Verses 10, 17, and 19 say her destruction occurred in one hour. It will not be a lengthy period.

More information about Babylon will be found in the Appendix.

Victory! (Revelation 19)

With eyes and ears, John had witnessed the end of Babylon, but there was more for him to know and record. He hears a loud voice from heaven. It is the voice of a great multitude singing "Alleluia"—praise to God for His judgments on the great harlot because of all she had done. John sees God's attendants, the twenty-four elders, and four heavenly beings fall prostrate in worship of God. A voice comes from the throne: "Praise our God all of you His servants, all you that fear Him, small and great." The great multitude responds with a voice of a mighty thundering, for it comes from people of many nations and languages. "Let us be glad and rejoice and give Him glory, for the marriage of the Lamb has come, and His wife has made herself ready."

John is overwhelmed. It seems so long since He heard Jesus tell His followers, "and you yourselves be like men who wait for their Lord when He shall return from the wedding" (Luke 12:36). He has been writing so much about the cruel, destructive work of Satan and his followers. He has heard repeated the human proverb, "the days are prolonged and every vision fails" (Ezek. 12:22). John is told, "Write, Blessed are those who are called to the marriage supper of the Lamb. These are the true sayings of God." At last, it is at hand. Such joy fills him that he has to worship. He falls at the feet of his angel messenger. He had to be reminded not to worship a fellow servant or a brother. He too rejoiced that he could bring such good news to John. He brought to John testimony from Jesus. It comes to humans through Christ's gift of prophecy. What comes through that gift is truth revealed by Jesus.

Then "heaven opened", and John witnessed a magnificent and wondrous panorama. The "Faithful and True" Savior and

Armageddon's Glorious End

Witness, Jesus Christ (Rev. 3:14), rides forth on a white horse. The language reminds us of the opening of the first seal, which pictured the apostles on a white horse going forth with the gospel to conquer (see Rev. 6:2). The sky is split apart. It is evident to all that the "King of kings and Lord of lords" has returned to earth in judgment. His eyes, as a flame of fire, make people realize He knows what they are. They have no place to hide. They cry out in despair (see Rev. 6:14–17).

He is clothed in a robe dipped in blood. What does that mean? Christians respond with the explanation that Christ gave His life to save us. That is a wonderful and true statement, but it touches only the surface of what our salvation cost. God loves people. He hates sin. What could He do when the people of His love embraced sin with its wage of death?

The words "For God so loved the world that He gave His only begotten Son that whoever believes in Him should not perish but have everlasting life" and "Christ loved us and gave Himself for us" come to mind as answers. Consider what the prophets Zechariah and Isaiah tell us is required and freely done by God. "In that day a fountain shall be opened for...sin and uncleanness." (Zech. 13:1, 6, 7). In providing the fountain, Messiah must accept being wounded by His people and friends, including me. He did this and then was able to pray, "Father forgive them."

"Awake O sword against My Shepherd, against the Man who is My Companion, says the Lord of Hosts. Strike the Shepherd and the sheep will be scattered." The Father must inflict the wages of sin upon the Son. It was as difficult for the Father to do that as it was for the Son to accept it. Each must agree: "Not My will but Thy will be done." The mystery of godliness was done, played out before the universe.

Add to this Isaiah 63:1–5. It tells of One in glorious apparel. He goes forth in the greatness of His strength. He is mighty to save. One look at Him answers the question, "Can He save a person like me?" The Holy Spirit answers, "He is able to do exceedingly abundantly above all that any human can ask or think." "He is able to save completely whoever will come to God through Him, since He ever lives to make intercession for them" (Eph. 3:20; Heb. 7:25).

Victory! (Revelation 19)

He has trodden the wine press of God's wrath alone. Of the people, there was no one with Him. In His humanity, Christ was strengthened to endure the agony of the "second death." His heart ruptured, and He died. His divinity, and also the Father, endured the second death suffering of the lost. I cannot explain it, nor will I try. I only know it is so. The cross is but a faint reflection to our dull senses of the pain that sin has caused to the heart of God since its very inception.

Revelation 19:19 refers to the war of Armageddon. Christ ends it. Verses 20 and 21 add to the information of the two harvests of 14:14–20. The beast and false prophet are captured and put into the lake of fire. Their history ends. Those organizations never appear again. All the rest of the unsaved are killed. They will appear in the second resurrection of chapter 20.

The Millenium (Revelation 20)

Chapter 20 opens with the earth desolated and void of people. The beast and false prophet were thrown into the lake of fire. The rest were slain. Other Bible passages agree that all the unbelievers will be destroyed when Christ returns to earth (see Matt. 13:30, 39–42; 2 Thess. 1:7–9; 2:8; also read Jeremiah 4:23–26 for a description of this earth after Jesus comes). That leaves only the dragon—Satan. He is bound to the destroyed surface of the earth. The plagues wreaked havoc on earth. The great hailstones and then the great earthquake that caused the mountains to disappear disrupted the entire surface.

Bottomless Pit

This term was used by the translators of the KJV for the Greek word *abyssos* ("without bottom"), from which we get the English "abyss." The Greek *abyssos* was used for the Hebrew word *tehom* by those who translated the Hebrew Scriptures into Greek. *Tehom* is found nineteen times in the Hebrew Old Testament. It is translated as "deep." The first time is Genesis 1:2: "The earth was without form and void and darkness was on the face of the deep" (*tehom*—"abyss").

The great earthquake (Rev. 6:14; 11:19; 16:18–20) completely mangles the earth. What kind of seismic action is it that makes the mountains disappear? Aftershocks continue. Volcano activity breaks forth in many places. The sky is so filled with debris and dust that darkness covers the earth until it is as described in Jeremiah 4:23–26.

Armageddon's Glorious End

Satan is bound with a chain. Jude 6 and 2 Peter 2:4 state that the angels that rebelled in heaven were cast down to *tartarus*—bound in chains of darkness for the judgment of the great day. How fitting this is for Satan. He who wanted to be as God (see Isa. 14:12–14, 17) ended up destroying the cities. To be God, one must be able to create. He has 1,000 years to do so. He cannot create a new earth. He can only nurse his anger and go insane with resentment.

Revelation 20 is the only place in the Bible that tells of the 1,000-year period. Why did John write about it? He was inspired by the Lord to do so. It was not a new idea. Various Jewish writers had written about it. For them, the 1,000 years was expected to begin about the time of Jesus. It would fulfill their hopes and bring the Messiah. The Lord used John to correct their ideas. It is Christ who brings the Millennium, not the Millennium that brings the Messiah (See Abba Hillel Silver's *A History of Messianic Speculation in Israel*, pp. 6, 7).

The details we find in verses 2–7 are:

The devil is bound at their beginning and remains bound for the 1,000 years.

Those who were killed for the testimony of Jesus, who would not worship the beast, its image, nor receive its mark, are brought to life and live and reign with Christ for the 1,000 years. "This is the first resurrection. They are blessed and holy." The rest of the dead, the unsaved, do not live again until the thousand years end. They will come under the "second death". Those in the first resurrection do not.

Here we have an example of how the Scriptures fit together. Revelation 19 pictures the victorious Christ coming to earth for His follower as He promised in John 14:1–3: "I will come again and receive you to Myself that where I am there you may be also." "Great is your reward in heaven" (Matt. 5:12). The earth cannot support life. Jesus takes the redeemed to heaven (see Matt. 24:30, 31; 1 Cor. 15:51–55; 1 Thess. 4:13–18).

During the millennium in heaven, the books are opened, and according to Romans 6:2–3, the saints "judge the world, even angels." Any questions the redeemed have will be answered.

The Millenium (Revelation 20)

Why are some people not there, and on what basis are others there? God created humans with a mind to think. He does not respond with "Don't question Me." All will be understood. Think how patiently God has been in carrying out His plan of salvation through centuries and millennia. It should not seem strange that He would give the redeemed 1,000 years to review and understand His judgment. The saints will see in each case the love and mercy of God. They will acclaim, "Righteous and true are you O Lord, because You have judged thus."

When the rest of the dead are raised at the end of the Millennium, Satan works to deceive them. He no doubt tells them that he has brought them to life and they can take the Holy City as it descends. Fire comes down from God out of heaven and devours them. This is the second death.

The fire purifies the earth. God makes the new heavens and new earth as He promised. Christ's other promise—"The meek shall inherit the earth"—is fulfilled.

The devil is cast into the lake of fire. Death and hell are cast into the lake of fire. The devil is not in charge of hell. The eternal fire was prepared for the devil and his angels (see Matthew 25:41).

"I will destroy you O covering cherub. Never shall you be any more" (Ezekiel 28:16, 19). Malachi 4:1–3 reads, "For behold the day is coming, burning like an oven, and all the proud, yes, all who do wickedly will be stubble. The day is corning says the Lord that will burn them up... that will leave them neither root nor branch... and they will be ashes under the soles of your feet."

Chapters 21 and 22 help us to picture the joys of eternal life and God's New Jerusalem.

The New Jerusalem (Revelation 21 and 22)

According to chapter 20, those redeemed from the earth "live and reign with Christ for 1,000 years and judgment was committed to them." What an experience it will be to review the cases of the saved and the lost! The character of God in His dealing with people is fully exposed. It is an experience that far surpasses Moses' experience when he requested that God "Show [him His] glory" (Exodus 33:18). The Lord replied that He would reveal all the glory that Moses could see without being consumed.

As the saints review the cases of individuals, the mercy of God and His continual, longsuffering, grace-giving work to bring people to salvation is present in every case. The glory of God is most evident in His sacrificial willingness to redeem the human race. His goodness and truth cannot be questioned in any case, even when the verdict of "guilty" had to be given. "God is good and He does good" (Ps. 119:68). To describe the redeemed as 100% committed to God is barely adequate. Describe it as you will—married to God, slaves to God, children of God—His name is on their forehead. "Never will evil again be manifest. Says the word of God, 'Affliction shall not rise up the second time.' Nahum 1:9...A tested and proved creation will never again be turned from allegiance to Him whose character has been fully manifested before them as fathomless love and infinite wisdom" (*The Great Controversy*, p. 504).

Revelation 21 and 22 tell of the new heaven and new earth which God had promised. Acts 3:20–21 refers to the many promises the Lord had given through the prophets. They pictured a bright future, but the things God had prepared for those who love Him will be more wonderful than anything we have seen; more breathtaking than any description we have heard; more awe-inspiring than anything our imagination can invent. "For I am persuaded that whatever we may have to go through now is less than nothing compared with the magnificent future God has planned for us. The whole creation is on tiptoe to see the wonderful sight of the sons of God coming into their own" (Rom. 8:18, 19, Phillips translation).

> *As the saints review the cases of individuals, the mercy of God and His continual, long suffering, grace-giving work to bring people to salvation is present in every case.*

"Behold! the tabernacle of God is with men, and He will dwell with them, and they shall be His people, and God Himself will be with them and be their God" (21:3). "They shall see His face. His name is on their foreheads" (22:4). The separation from the presence of God that was caused when Adam and Eve took their faith from God's words and put it in the words of the serpent is ended. Those who are saved will experience the reality that "In Your presence is fullness of joy; At Your right hand are pleasures forevermore" (Psalm 16:11, NKJV). "Every tear is wiped away, there is no more death, no more sorrow, no more crying, never will there be any pain." Those former things were in "the cup" and swallowed down by Christ. Never more will they exist.

The city has no need of the sun or the moon to shine in it, for the glory of God illuminates it, and the Lamb is its light. There is no night there. There is the Tree of Life from which to eat and the water of life from which to drink. Sickness and death are impossible (21:4, 6; 22:1–5). Several of the descriptions given in these two chapters are given as the fulfillment of what was prophesied by Ezekiel in chapters 28, 42, and 48.

The Bride, The Lamb's Wife

Revelation 19:7–8 present the bride as a person: "His bride has made herself ready." Corinthians 11:2 uses the same symbolism of people being the bride: "That I may present you as a chaste virgin to Christ." Revelation 21:9–10 identifies His bride as the New Jerusalem. This is not a contradiction. In Revelation, Babylon and the New Jerusalem appear as rivals for two opposing kingdoms. Eight times in Revelation, Babylon is called "that great city", but Babylon is not a geographical place; it is a confederacy of peoples.

The New Jerusalem, "that great city" which John was shown "descending out of heaven from God" will be a geographical place. At the same time, it symbolizes God's redeemed people. Its foundations bear the names of the twelve apostles who Christ used to establish His church. To enter the city, one goes through its gates as a member of the twelve tribes. This shows the unity of God's work of salvation both before and after Christ's earthly life and ministry. All the redeemed become one in Christ (of whom the whole family in heaven and earth is named). "The Jerusalem above is free, she is the mother of us all" (Eph. 3:15; Gal. 4:26).

City walls were of great importance in those centuries. Walls were vital. They promised safety and security for a city's inhabitants. Isaiah 60 pictures the time when the Redeemer shall come to Zion, and that "Violence shall no longer be heard in your land... You shall call your walls Salvation, and your gates Praise. The sun shall no longer be your light by day... The Lord will be to you an everlasting light'" (vs. 18, 19, NKJV). The gates of the New

Jerusalem are never shut. There is no danger or evil to shut out; nothing from which to be protected. This fulfills Zechariah 2:4: "Jerusalem shall be inhabited as towns without walls... For I says the Lord will be a wall of fire all around her. I will be the glory in her midst." The walls and gates exist for the glory and beauty of the city.

The way the bride is presented fits the marriage and wedding customs of that time. Jesus, instructing His disciples about His return to earth, told them to be like men who wait for their Lord when He shall return from the wedding (see Luke 12:36). Christ's right to reclaim the lost dominion was made official in heaven. It is pictured in Daniel 7:13–14: "One like the Son of Man came before the Ancient of Days and there was given to Him dominion, glory and a kingdom, that all peoples, nations and languages should serve Him." Recall Satan's words to Jesus when he tempted Him. Satan showed Jesus all the kingdoms of the world, with the claim, "all this has been delivered to me." It was true. By the choice Adam and Eve made to listen to Satan's lies, the dominion that had been theirs was passed to him. Christ came to break his claim.

Christ did not bargain with Satan, for that would have justified his claims. Christ's life revealed the righteousness and love of God. His life and teaching disproved all the claims Satan made against God. Christ defeated Satan. By His death, the Righteous One provided forgiveness and salvation for all who would put their faith in Him as their Savior. As Jacob, by his seven years of labor for Rachel, earned her to be his wife, Jesus, by the life He lived and the death He died, purchased His bride. He is the "kinsman Redeemer." Heaven's judgment (see Dan. 7) declares the righteousness of what He has done, and the Bridegroom comes for His bride.

One must read the description of the city for oneself. For me, it is beyond anything I can fathom. "The city was pure gold, like clear glass." I have not seen such gold; the twelve foundations, each one a jewel and adorned with all kinds of precious stones; each gate a pearl. I am full of wonder. Sometimes when I drive along Watts Bar Lake in Kingston, Tennessee, the angle of the sun makes the water dance and sparkle brilliantly as if jewels were

The Bride, The Lamb's Wife

spread all over the surface of the water. It makes me wonder if we will need dark glasses to look at the Holy City.

Revelation 22:6–21 gives the conclusion of the book which Christ instructed John to write. The events written are "faithful and true." They are sure to happen. Again, the wonder of it all was so overwhelming that John had to worship. To read and grasp what is being revealed will lead us to do the same.

"Behold I am coming quickly. Blessed is the person who keeps the words of the prophecy of this book." "And behold I am coming quickly, and My reward is with Me to give to everyone according to his work." "I Jesus have sent My angel to testify to you these things in the churches..." "Surely I am coming quickly" (vs. 7, 12, 16, 20). Bible prophecy makes it clear that we are living in "the time of the end", the "last days". In place of the word "quickly", use the word "suddenly", for His return occurs when popular thinking is that 'It has been so long, nothing will happen now.' At such a time "the Son of Man comes" (Mark 13:36; 1 Thess. 5:3; Matt. 24:44).

Jesus, "the Alpha and Omega, the Beginning and the End, the First and the Last", who became the promised "Root and Offspring of David, the Bright and Morning Star", pleads with every reader of His book: "keep the words of this prophecy." Do not let anyone change its meaning or tell you that you do not need to worry about its message.

The Lord's final blessing is given in verse 14. Two readings are found in ancient manuscripts: "Blessed are those who do His commandments, that they may have right to the Tree of Life and may enter through the gates into the city" and "Blessed are those who have washed their robes in the blood of the Lamb that they may have right to the Tree of Life and enter through the gates into the city." The two readings do not deny each other. The "white robes" of the redeemed are referred to in Revelation 3:4, 5, 18, 4:4, 6:11, and 7:9, 13, and 14. To suggest that those who have washed their robes and made them white in the blood of the Lamb are free to ignore and disobey God's law makes no sense.

Revelation 12:17 and 14:12 tell us that God's people "keep the commandments of God." Revelation 21:27 and 22:15 tell us that those who disobey God's law will never enter The New Jerusalem. They exclude themselves from salvation.

"Come!" calls Jesus. "Come!" pleads the Spirit. "I want My children home" speaks the Father. "Come with us!" urges His people. All the blessings of this book, all the promises of God, are for you too.

John's Story — Revelation as Narrative

The idea that Revelation contains a story may strike one as an odd thought, but it does. It is much more than a series of strange visions. It is a book with a purpose. It continues the story of Jesus Christ in His work to bring to completion God's great purpose for this world (see Isa. 45:18; Acts 3:20, 21). Revelation gives us a preview of gospel history.

The four Gospels present Jesus from His birth to His death, resurrection, and ascension. From Acts to Jude we have the story of Christ's followers in the first century. These are not biographies. Rather, they are stories whose purpose is to bring people to faith in the Lord Jesus Christ. In them, we see how God built His church in this world.

Revelation reveals events that begin during the time of John and continue through Christian history to the return of Christ, and then the establishment of God's New Jerusalem in this world (however, the book does not give us a one-line chronology of events). Humans have given this book the title: "The Revelation of John", but that is not what it is. John is not the author. It came from God. It is "the revealing of (the victorious) Jesus Christ." It was brought by Christ's angel to His bondservant, John. John is the scribe. In obedience to Christ, John wrote the story (Rev. 1:1, 2).

John begins his writing as he began his Gospel and first letter. Not with his name, but with Christ—God—the Word. God is the great Reality of all life and human hope. John, the last survivor of the twelve apostles, does not talk about himself. He, who, with his brother James, once desired the highest positions with Christ, has changed. He has no desire to promote himself. He knew he could not forgive sins. He could not change lives. Only Jesus can do that. John simply says, "I, your brother and fellow partaker in tribulation... was on the island of Patmos, because of the word of God and the testimony of Jesus" (v. 9). Why wasn't John killed like Stephen, his brother James, Peter, Paul, and so many others were? Emperor Domitian, who demanded that he be worshipped as "Lord and God" was responsible for many deaths. Tradition tells us that Rome had tried to kill John, but failed. They could only exile him to Patmos.

What a story John could have told! He could have, with true drama, told of being arrested and condemned to death. With great fanfare, as a warning to Christians, he was put in a vat of boiling oil. He stood in the oil. Nothing harmed him. What consternation must have filled the lives of the emperor, soldiers, and all those gloating over the occasion! What notoriety! We, today, would take such an occasion to attract an audience. John did no such thing. His brother James had not been delivered. Too many Christians were suffering and had been killed for him to magnify his deliverance. John the Apostle, like John the Baptist, knew "He must increase, I must decrease." There is no greater calling or honor than, as His bondservant, to testify of Jesus Christ.

John could recall when older brother James and he, there by Lake Galilee, were called by the Messiah to follow Him. They, the thunder brothers, willingly became His disciples. He could remember the Messianic hopes they then cherished—the overthrow of Roman rule and Israel becoming first among the nations. How shortsighted they were. Messiah had accomplished so much more than they had then imagined. In the seed promised to Abraham, Isaac, Jacob, and David, "all the families of the earth were blessed."

John now knows that he and all believers are bound to God by the "new," the everlasting Covenant, which was effected in Christ. "He bought us with a price." The price was His own life. "He washed us from our sins in His own blood, and made us a kingdom of priests to our God." (Rev. 1:5, 6)

John's Story — Revelation as Narrative

John had been with Jesus throughout His ministry. He had witnessed all the events from Jesus' baptism to His ascension to heaven. He was among the three disciples that Christ occasionally singled out for special experiences with Him. John saw so much. He felt closer to Christ than the rest did. Thinking back, John could remember Jesus words: "O you of little faith, why did you doubt?" He could also remember their "slowness to believe all that the prophets had spoken" and the putting out of mind any words about His coming death. John has put that all behind. Doubts and fears no longer assail him. Christ is too faithful for any doubts. What Christ says, happens.

Jerusalem's beautiful temple was gone. John could recall when the disciples had pointed to its great beauty and strength and the questions that swarmed in their minds when Jesus said, "Not one stone will be left on another." What Jesus said, happened. Faithful Christians had fled the city. Now the "Faithful and True Witness" was giving further information. It is information that was to guide His people from that day until the glorious day when He comes with clouds, and every eye beholds Him (see 1:7; 22:12). "I was in the Spirit on the Lord's day." John's thoughts were of Jesus. Revelation 1:7 makes us think that John may have been repeating the words of Jesus, which we read in Matthew 24:30–31, for the language is so similar

> *John has put that all behind. Doubts and fears no longer assail him. Christ is too faithful for any doubts. What Christ says, happens.*

How had John been spending that Sabbath day? The way that Jesus did. During the years the disciples had spent with Jesus, they had experienced Sabbath in a new way. His Sabbath-keeping was different from that required by Pharisees. Christ said, "the Sabbath was made for man." It was a gift of God for the human race, not man offering something to God. Its purpose was to keep people connected to their Creator. When Jesus declared "the Son of Man is Lord of the Sabbath," the claim was shocking, but now

John and other Christians understood it. They kept the Sabbath according to the Lord's life. They did not "sabbatize" as the Jews insisted.

Cut off from fellowship with any church, and aware of their persecution, he must have been praying for the believers. His faith lifted him above his circumstances so he could sing and rejoice in Christ. His keepers could not help but respect this aged "saint" whose kind ways and concern for them were such a puzzle. They heard the reports of his deliverance, and the common belief in the supernatural must have caused them to look at him with awe. How else could he have the means of writing out the visions?

Then John received a Sabbath blessing that has never been equaled. His Master, who in His earthly life, met with His people on the Sabbath day, taught them and worked miracles for them, came and met with John (see Isa. 58:13).

He gave him teachings for His church through the end of time and worked the miracle of enabling John to witness and write all that he saw. God spoke to John the words: "I am the Alpha and the Omega, the Lord God, who is and was and is to come, the Almighty", and John was in vision. John heard a loud voice, like a trumpet. He was told, "to write in a book all that he saw and to send it to the seven named churches" (1:8, 10, 11). That "loud voice like a trumpet" is a summons to all the earth "to hear what the Spirit revealed." "All you inhabitants of the world and dwellers on earth... as soon as the trumpet is blown you will hear it" (Isa. 45:3). Christ's voice, like a trumpet, is to be heard. His church is to make it known. "None of the wicked will understand, but the wise will understand" (Dan. 12:10; Matt. 24:14; Rev. 10:11; 14:6, 7; 22:17).

The voice came from behind him, so John turned to see who was speaking. In turning, he first saw lampstands. As the whole scene came into view, he saw in the middle of the seven lamps the Son of Man. There is no question about John's meaning for this title. John uses it frequently in his Gospel. It was Christ's favorite title for Himself. Its origin is found in Genesis 3:15. Not some mythological god, or an angel from heaven, but One born into the human race, "a Son of Man", would crush the serpent's head.

John's Story — Revelation as Narrative

Jesus, who gave Himself to the human race, maintains His glorified humanity, so John, who "had seen and handled Him", recognized Him. At the same time, John saw Him with all the attributes which, in the Old Testament, are descriptions of God (vs. 13–16; Dan. 7:9; 10:6; Ezek. 43:2; Isa. 11:4). The glory which Christ had with the Father before the world was is revealed. No wonder John fell down as dead. We will also respond to His mighty saving presence. The awe and wonder we will experience cannot be described. John reports, "He laid His right hand on me"—that is, the hand of favor and blessing. Christ said, "Do not be afraid." At those recreative words, new life came into John.

Christ did not stop there. He said more: "I am the First and the Last." Eternity exists in Him. "I am the living One." He is the life-giving One. "He who has the Son has eternal life. He who has not the Son does not have eternal life" (1 Jon. 5:11, 12). Christ "has the keys of death and Hades." Satan would not open the house of his prisoners (see Isa. 14:17). Jesus, in His life, "overcame the strong man, and plundered his house" (Matt. 12:29).

By the life He lived, He overcame all sin and Satan. He died in our place, but "it was not possible for death to hold Him" (Acts 2:24). The way the empty tomb was left, with folded grave clothes, witnesses that His exit was not a flight. He is in charge of the tomb. Christ tore off the gate of death and left it on Calvary's hill beneath His cross.

People die. Some specifically are put to death for their faith. However, all like Lazarus are only asleep (see John 11:11–26; 1 Thess. 4:13–18). They will rise again. No devil, man, or any priest can take the keys from deity.

"The Lord is for me, I will not fear what man can do to me" (Psalm 118:6). With settled assurance and great enthusiasm, John began to write. The churches must see the victorious Christ of Revelation. The churches must know the things which would come to pass.

Did John understand all that He saw and wrote? No, he could not understand all that was signified by the visions he recorded. However, that was alright, for just as he and the other disciples had eventually come to understand all that Jesus had taught, so

God in His own time would cause His people to understand these visions.

Neither was John given an explanation of how all that God showed to him would be accomplished. He did not need it. What he saw and heard in Christ—His baptism, life, teachings, miracles, death, resurrection, ascension, and the gift of the Holy Spirit—made John know that whatever else Christ revealed of things to come would definitely occur.

The visions revealed that great dangers were ahead. Satan would work every way possible to destroy Christ's church and gospel. However, Jesus is "in the midst of His people. He holds His faithful messengers in His right hand." "I have told you before it comes to pass, that when it comes to pass you may believe" (John 14:29). Christ would enable His church to discern the events and proclaim His heaven-sent messages.

God's purpose would be accomplished in the earth. The triumph of the Lamb had made certain the triumph of His church (see Matt. 27:50–52; Rev. 5).

> *God's purpose would be accomplished in the earth. The triumph of the Lamb had made certain the triumph of His church.*

He is coming again! "Behold I make all things new." Christ will have "a great number which no one can count." God's New Jerusalem will come down upon this earth. "God Himself will be with us." "I am coming quickly." "Amen, come Lord Jesus" (Rev. 7:9; 21:2, 3, 5; 22:20).

Thank you, Lord Jesus! And thank you, John, for your faithful ministry. "These things have been written that you might believe that Jesus is the Christ, the Son of God, and that believing you may have life in His name" (John 20:31). "This is the victory that overcomes the world—our faith" (1 John 5:4).

Appendix

Final Events

A Survey of the Book of Revelation

Things to Know When Reading Revelation

Silence in Heaven—The Seventh Seal

The Real Conspiracy

The Prophetic Beasts of Daniel 7, 8, and Revelation 13

Mark of the Beast–2

A Further Understanding of Babylon in Revelation

The Abomination of Desolation (Matthew 24:15; Mark 13:14)

The Lord's Supper

The Emphasis of the New Testament

Messiah, and the Israel of God

The Nature of the Church, its Government, and Mission

This I Know—God is for Me

Speaking as a Serpent

Why would a Christian Worship on Saturday?

Appendix

Final Events

The purpose of prophecy is to build our faith and draw us near to Christ (see 2 Pet. 1:19). Matthew 24 is a good place to start the study of final events. As Jesus left the temple (see Matt. 23: 38, 39), He said, "Your house is left to you desolate. You will not see me until you shall say, 'Blessed is he who comes in the name of the Lord." His disciples were perplexed. The temple was the center of Jewish national life. He said it would be left desolate. Three days earlier, a crowd had escorted Jesus, shouting the words "Hosanna to the son of David, blessed is He that comes in the name of the Lord", the very words to which Jesus referred. Later, when they pointed to the magnificent buildings of the temple mount, Christ replied that it would all be destroyed (Matt. 21:8, 9; 24:1, 2).

> *The purpose of prophecy is to build our faith and draw us near to Christ.*

Imagine the disciples trying to fit together their hope of the Messiah's kingdom with Christ's words. Jesus had proclaimed, "The kingdom of heaven is near," and told the disciples to proclaim it. Now Jesus spoke of the destruction of the temple and Jerusalem. Jesus retired to the Mount of Olives. His disciples came to Him with their questions. "When will these things be?" What things? The destruction of Jerusalem and His coming to which He referred as He left the temple (see Matt. 24:3).

In His discourse, Jesus answered both questions. Specific events which Jesus foretold were fulfilled in the war that resulted in the destruction of Jerusalem by General Titus in A.D. 70. When the Roman armies withdrew from their siege, Christians fled the city as Jesus had instructed (see Matt. 24:16–18). They were not in darkness that that day caught them unprepared. The Roman army returned, and those who believed the city was their protection were killed or enslaved.

As surely as Christ's words about the temple came to pass, so His words about His coming will be fulfilled. Fulfilled prophecy in the past builds our faith to trust and obey His teaching as we live for His appearing. "Watch, and be ready, for in a time when people are focused on other hopes, the Son of man will come." (Matt. 24:43, 44, paraphrased)

The words Christ gave in Matthew 24 describe life in the final age—wars, famines, earthquakes, persecution of His followers, deadly diseases, floods, fires, tornadoes, etc.; lawlessness increasing until the earth is "as in the days of Noah", filled with self-indulgent sexual pleasure, anger, and unrestrained violence. In looking at America and the world, we have to admit it is a true prophecy. Jesus gave no picture of humans establishing God's kingdom on earth. Humans do not bring in the millennium.

Three times in His instruction, Jesus spoke of false prophets and Christs (see vs. 5, 11, 23–27). This underscores the importance of holding to clear Bible teachings and not being swayed by human reasoning or miracles that support teachings contrary to the Bible.

When one supplements the study of Matthew 24 with references to 2 Corinthians 11:13–15, 2 Thessalonians 2:9,10, 1 Timothy 4:1, and Revelation 13:12–15 and 16:13–14, it becomes very evident that in the last days, signs, wonders, and miracles will be used to deceive the world and substitute human laws in place of God's law. Peter, John, Paul, and Jude, in their letters, mention false teachers. The warnings about false teachings are needed. We are to "try the spirits...". However, there is still a danger.

That danger is seen in Christ's words to the church of Ephesus (see Rev. 2:2–6). The Ephesians discerned between truth and falsehood and good and evil behavior. The error of Ephesus was that it had "lost its first love." Love for their Savior and other people was replaced by suspicion of others. Christians are not called to be detectives hunting for error. We are called to be witnesses for Christ and to seek and to save the lost. Jesus spoke

Final Events

of their hatred of the deeds of the Nicolaitans. The people were not to be hated, only their deeds. If we lose our love for Christ and exercise no labor of love for the people around us to be saved, we are in danger of being removed. This is one reason why John wrote so much about brotherly love in his letters.

FINAL EVENTS: In addition to natural disasters, increasing lawlessness, and all types of error being taught, other specific events are declared in the Bible:

"Daniel...seal the book until the time of the end, knowledge shall be increased and many will run to and fro" (Daniel 12:4). Never has knowledge and technology increased as it has today. Unfortunately, there have also been many negative increases: fearful sights and great signs from heaven; nations in distress; fearfulness of the future; unmitigated anger; terrorism; strife between rich and poor groups (see Luke 21:11, 25–27; James 5:1–3).

"This gospel shall be preached... then shall the end come" (Matt. 24:14). Christ gave to His church what we call "The Great Commission" (see Matt. 28:18–20). This is the mission for every follower of Christ—"to seek and save the lost." The messenger of Revelation 14:6 has the eternal gospel. It is preached all over the world. It announces that God's redemption is reaching its climax. The "hour of God's judgment is come." It is the "Elijah" call to repentance and holy living to prepare people for the Lord. The gospel is the power of God for salvation to those who believe (see Romans 1:17). It is the saving power of Jesus Christ that produces people who "keep the commandments of God and the faith of Jesus" (Rev. 14:12).

The three angels' messages bring the harvest of the earth (see Rev. 14:14–20). Modem technology enables the gospel to be sent through the heavens and all over the world. Just as it is depicted in Revelation 14:6, this final event is being accomplished.

These heaven-sent messages for earth's last days call people to "worship Him who created all things." Babylon is fallen and does not speak for God. To worship—to obey—the teaching of the beast and its image causes one to receive the wrath of God. These words take one back to Revelation 12 and 13, where the mark of the beast with its worship is introduced. (see Dan. 7, 8, and 9 and 2 Thess. 2:1–9 for more background).

True worship (John 4:23, 24) versus false worship is the issue presented in Revelation. To live and teach the truth as it is in Jesus is our calling.

A Survey of the Book of Revelation

Its title is "The Revelation of John", but that is not what it is. John is the writer, but not the author. It came from God. It begins with the words "the revelation of Jesus Christ." It was brought by an angel to John, Christ's bondservant.

Consider John. He identifies himself and all Christians as "bondservants". We are bound to God by His "new" everlasting covenant, which was effected in Christ. He bought us with a price. The price was His own life. "He washed us from our sins in His own blood and has made us a kingdom of priests to our God" (Rev. 1:5, 6. NASB). Revelation proclaims the gospel in all its completeness.

John, the last survivor of the twelve apostles, was a prisoner of Rome in exile. He writes, "I, your brother and fellow partaker in tribulation, and in the kingdom and patience of Jesus Christ, was on the Island of Patmos, because of the word of God and the testimony of Jesus" (v. 9). In vision, John "Heard behind [him] a loud voice like the sound of a trumpet." When he turned to see the source of the voice, he saw "one like the Son of Man." It was not an angel. It was a man, but such a man. A man who was also deity (vs. 12–15).

John had walked with Jesus. He had talked with Him. He looked upon Him day after day, put his hands on Him, and leaned upon His chest. However, now John fell as dead before Him. What else could any human do? During Christ's earthly ministry, the disciples had difficulty grasping that the man they believed to be the Messiah was, from the beginning, God.

John was told to write in a book the things he saw and heard. Revelation is one book. It is not seven books or two books, but one. The whole book is for the church (see Rev. 22:16). It begins with the time of John and closes with all evil gone and all things made new.

"The Revelation of Jesus Christ" presents to us Christ in His victory. He was victorious over sin (see Rev. 1:5). He was victorious over death (see Rev. 1:18). He was victorious over Satan, the father of all evil (see Rev. 12:12). All the promises of God are sealed for fulfillment in Him (see 2 Cor. 1:19, 20). As a Conqueror, claiming the fruits of His victory, He is at the throne of God (see Rev. 5).

> *In Revelation, Christ unmasks Satan's attempt to undermine His salvation.*

In Revelation, Christ unmasks Satan's attempt to undermine His salvation. He works to destroy, or take over and use for his purposes, the gospel and the church. This warfare is revealed in the persecution that John and other Christians were experiencing.

In this controversy, Revelation initially pictures heaven's activity as worked out on earth. Then we find a presentation of satanically inspired activity.

Chapter 1—Heaven sends a message to earth. Heavenly activity involving the Father, Son, and the Holy Spirit, brings the Revelation to earth. John, a human, must write it out and distribute it.

Chapters 2 and 3—The seven churches represent the church throughout the Christian era. Christ's first concern is His church which He builds and guards. What is depicted is the human activity that occurs in the churches. By His Word and Spirit, Christ worked to keep His church faithful to Him. The warnings and reproofs given to the seven churches reveal that Christianity was being infiltrated with error, as well as being persecuted. There were always those who "heard what the Spirit said to the church." They remained faithful. There were many who continued in the errors that were pointed out and led Christianity away from Christ.

A Survey of the Book of Revelation

Chapters 4 and 5—A scene from the throne of heaven. Here is heavenly activity, and this activity is all part of God's great work to bring people to salvation. From the time of Adam on through the centuries, God had given prophecies that told of restoration, no more curse of sin, no more tears, and all things made new.

How could the promises be brought to reality? Who could redeem the lost inheritance? The deed was closed and sealed. How could holiness embrace the human race in its wickedness? How could the glorious future promised by God and written down by the prophets ever come to be?

Are we humans left to weep, as did John, over the sealed scroll? Is it never to become a reality? Weep not! The Promised One, "The Lion of Judah" and "The Root of David" has prevailed. He sits at God's right hand. All God's promises are in Him and will become a reality on earth. Heaven is at work to bring it to pass.

Jesus Christ is the center of human history. He, in a new powerful way, brought life and the wisdom of God into the world. His life reveals that the major dilemma for the human race is its separation from God. Without Him, its future is sin, decay, and death. Christ reunites humanity to God, life, and a glorious future. He provides the only solution for us and our problems. To wait and expect that God has yet to perform some great act in the world and then people will be changed and all will be peace is a deception. God's great act of salvation has been done in Christ. Human pride ignores this truth and attempts to provide a man-made solution for the world.

Chapter 6 presents events on earth. Six seals are opened. Christianity as a kingdom or represented by society changes from the apostolic church to an imperial papacy. The seven seals and subsequent chapters reveal more about "the falling away" (2 Thess. 2:1–12), persecutions, and "isms" at work to destroy God's people and truth.

Chapter 7 answers the question, "Who shall be able to stand" (Rev. 6:17)? Heaven's activity on earth enables His servants to receive the seal of God.

Chapters 8 and 9—The trumpets signal events on earth that brought about the destruction of the Roman Empire. This enabled the development of the imperial papacy. Then came the rise of Islam. These political events should be considered from the viewpoint of how they impacted the gospel and Christianity.

Revelation 10:1–11:1 pertains to heaven's activity on earth. The little book being opened led to the widespread study and teaching that, according to Daniel's prophecies, Christ's return was at hand.

Revelation 11:2–14 deals with The French Revolution, which was fueled by The Enlightenment and the oppressive rule of church and privileged class over the common people. The rise of the worship of reason led to naturalism, atheism, and evolution. For many, faith in God and the Bible had been eclipsed.

Verses 15–19 emphasize that looking to Christ and His ministry in heaven's temple is a necessary preparation for His people.

Chapter 12—Here is revealed what is behind all the activity on earth. It is Satan's constant war against God and His work of salvation. Satan was not able to defeat the "Manchild", so he continues his war to destroy God's truth and people. Revelation 12:17 introduces us to Satan's final war against Christ's "remnant" who hold to the teaching of Jesus, not human interpretations. They are especially guided by the testimony Christ gives in the book of Revelation and by His Spirit. They do not regard Revelation as too difficult to understand or not vital to Christianity. It gives to them direction and certainty. God's people are identified as keeping His commandments (see Rev. 12:17; 14:12).

Chapter 13 reflects human activity on earth, inspired by Satan. Here is presented how Satan makes war against the remnant. He will bring about the issue of "The mark of the beast". This final apostasy in Christendom constitutes the "third woe" for the earth. The worship prescribed by the beast and its image remains the dividing issue through the rest of Revelation (see 13:15; 14:9–12: 15:2; 16:2, 10; 17:3, 8; 19:20; 20:4).

Chapter 14 depicts more heavenly activity. The victorious remnant is portrayed. Then is presented the heavenly activity that made them victorious. It was by accepting and sharing the messages of the "three angels" that they kept faithful and true to God. These messages, in conflict with the message of the beast

A Survey of the Book of Revelation

and his image, make the harvest of the earth fully ripe. Heaven reaps earth's harvest.

Chapters 15 and 16 highlight heavenly activity of a different nature than before. All the previous activity of heaven was to bring people to salvation. The time arrives when no one can enter the temple; the day of salvation has passed (see Heb. 6:18–20). The plagues begin the execution of heavenly judgment on Babylon. The righteousness of God's judgment is declared.

Chapter 17—Babylon's work is what brought the plagues. Heaven gives information that further enables the people of God to understand and to identify the final Babylon and the confederacy that constitutes it (see 13:2, 11; 16:13, 14; 17:12–16). The plagues cause this union to crumble, and they turn on each other.

Chapter 18:1–4—Here is heaven's inspired work that closed the giving of the three angels' messages. This reminds us that before sending His judgments, God does everything possible to bring people to repentance and salvation.

Verses 5–19 describe the collapse of Babylon, but mainly in economic terms. The global economy is devastated. Today it is evident that it is the economy that unites the nations of the earth to work together. We also experience how disasters and greed affect economic stability, which is so important to society. Because of the plagues, business is left in shambles.

In chapter 19, heaven acts. Jesus comes to receive His bride. The beast and false prophet are cast into the lake of fire. All followers of Babylon are slain. Armageddon ends.

Chapter 20 depicts the earth as Satan and sin have made it to be—utterly broken down and desolate. Satan is confined to it for 1,000 years. Does he come to his senses and admit his sin and rebellion? He, who wanted to be God, has no ability to be God. He cannot create the world anew. He has no life in himself to make people live. How could he imagine himself to be God? Will he admit his wrong? No. As soon as he is released, he goes out still attempting to destroy.

Christ's redeemed people are with Him in heaven. They review the judgment. They are able to see and learn all that heaven was doing for them, their loved ones, and all humanity. They conclude that the second death is the only solution that their Lord Jesus Christ has for the rest of the dead.

Chapters 21 and 22 highlight the New Jerusalem on the new earth. God dwells with His redeemed people. The event promised, hoped for, looked for, and was made possible by the life and death of Jesus, becomes a reality!

Things to Know When Reading Revelation

The events given in Revelation begin with the time of John and close with all things made new. John was told to "write in a book" what he was shown and send it to the seven churches. It is one book, not seven books. There is a unity in its structure.

It begins and closes with identical thoughts: The entire book is for the church (1:4; 22:16). Revelation begins with a blessing for the person who reads, hears, and keeps the things that are written in this prophecy and ends with the same blessing (l:3; 22:7). Christ had promised, "I will come again" (John 14:3). This promised event is repeated in Revelation 1:7 and 22:7, 12 and 20.

The visions given do not present one single chronology of events. In Revelation, as in the prophecies of Daniel, the Lord presents some truth in a vision and then adds more to it in subsequent visions. It presents several groups of prophecies. The groups run parallel to each other. They reinforce and expand Christ's prophetic picture of the age-long conflict between Christ and Satan. They all lead to the return of Christ in power and glory.

The event of Christ's return is found in each of the vision groups. It is mentioned in Jesus' message to Philadelphia, the sixth of the seven churches (see 3:11). The sixth seal presents how His coming brings terror to the world (see 6:14–17).

Following the vision of the seals comes the vision of the seven trumpets (see 8:6–11:17). After the sixth trumpet comes the mighty, heavenly message: "time no more shall be" (10:6, 7). Prophecy is being fulfilled. The day is near, but "you must prophesy again"

(10:11). The sounding of the seventh trumpet brings another picture of "the end" (Rev. 11:15–19).

Revelation 12–14 is another group of visions. Chapter 12 depicts Satan and his age-long war against God. Since the victory of the promised "man-child", Satan has intensified his work. He works through the beast powers (chapter 13) to destroy God's truth and people. Revelation 14:1–12 shows God's people and the messages that kept them faithful.

Revelation 14:13–20 pictures the harvest of the earth. "The harvest is the end of the world" (Matt. 13:39). This is the third time Revelation pictures the end. Following the seventh plague, the end of this world is again presented (see 16:17–21).

The final portrayal of Christ's coming is in Revelation 19:11–21. There we see Jesus Christ in glorious majesty, "King of kings, and Lord of lords." The beast and false prophet are thrown into the lake of fire, and all who follow them are killed.

The visions do not present a one-line chronology. They give the understanding which the church needs to not be deceived by Satan, keep faithful to God, and fulfill its mission in giving the message of Christ to all the earth.

Silence in Heaven— The Seventh Seal

"When the Lamb opened the seventh seal, there was silence in heaven for about half an hour" (Rev 8:1). What could this mean? From the beginning, God has been in communication with the human race. "Where are you, Adam? I have saving news for you" (see Gen. 3:8, 9, 15). God spoke through the prophets. Finally, He spoke through the Son (see Heb. 1:1, 2). There on Patmos, the Son, by His Spirit, was speaking to John and, by extension, all Christians.

He still speaks. In heaven, Christ is at the throne of God, and as our Mediator He speaks for us and to us. "The Spirit and the bride say, Come." "Today, if you will hear His voice harden not your hearts." "Refuse not Him who speaks from heaven" (Heb. 3:7–15; 12:25–27; Rev. 22:16–20).

Revelation 10 and 14:6–12 tell us that heaven speaks to earth, declaring that "time no more shall be" and "the hour of God's judgment is come." "Worship Him who created", not the beast and his mark. Heaven is not yet silent. With great authority and glory, heaven speaks (see Rev. 18:1–4). This is the issue to which the human race is brought. God's remnant people of faith are His human voice that proclaim the Word from heaven.

When, in opposition to God's Word, the mark of the beast is enforced under penalty of death, heaven will go silent. Intercession for sinners will end. "No man can enter the temple" (Rev. 15:8). Christ no longer mediates His blood in God's presence for humanity. The Holy Spirit no longer pleads "Come!" The words of Revelation 22:11 and 12 have been pronounced. Sinners have

Armageddon's Glorious End

grieved away the Holy Spirit. They will feel as Jesus did when He cried out on the cross, "My God, My God why have You forsaken Me?" (Matt. 27:46) "The people will stagger from sea to sea, and from the north to the east; they will go to and fro to seek the word of the Lord, but they will not find it" (Amos 8:11, 12).

When Christ was brought before King Herod, He gave him the rebuke of silence. Herod had killed God's messenger, John the Baptist. Heaven had no more to say to him. The passing of the death decree against those who refuse to worship the beast and its image seals the world's fate. Heaven goes silent, leaving the world to experience life as it has chosen it to be. The seven last plagues fall upon the world (see Rev. 16).

For God's people, this is the time of "Jacob's trouble" (Jer. 30:5–7). "Jacob's trouble" refers to the experience of Jacob. He, in obedience to God's instruction, was returning to the promised land. He learned that his brother Esau was coming and, remembering Esau's vow to kill him, he did not know what to do. In his fear and distress, he pled with God and "wrestled with the angel." Out of his struggle of faith with God, deliverance came. He was given a new name—Israel (Israel was not given to be an ethnic name. It is the name for God's people of faith. It symbolizes the new name Christ gives to the overcomers).

"O God do not remain quiet: Do not be silent, and O my God do not be still. For behold Your enemies make an uproar! And those who hate You have exalted themselves. They make shrewd plans against Your people, and conspire against Your treasured ones. They have said, 'Come, let us wipe them out as a nation'" (Ps. 83:1–4, NASB; see also Rev. 13:1).

This war against Christ and His true worship is the climax of Armageddon. The harvest of the earth is ripe (see Rev. 14:13–20).

This "half hour" experience of silence demonstrates what sin does and what humans are when they are unsheltered and unrestrained by the grace of God. The winds of human passions are let loose (see Rev. 7:1, 2). The plagues fall, causing a time of trouble, greater and more appalling than the world has ever known (see Dan. 12:1).

It also demonstrates that God's salvation in Christ can restore His people to complete unity with Him. Under the threat of death,

Silence in Heaven—The Seventh Seal

they are tested as Jacob was tested, but heavenly angels guard them. Like Job, they may suffer the loss of all earthly support, but by the blood of the Lamb they keep "the faith of Jesus." Like Job, their faith says, "Though He slay me, yet will I trust Him" (Jer. 30:7; Rev. 13:10; 14:12; Job 13:15).

Many Christians have a weak understanding of what God's grace does. They believe it forgives their sin, but not that it can "keep [them] from falling." Jesus saves us "from our sins", not "in our sins." Can God's grace restore to the condition where, if one was placed in Eden, as were Adam and Eve, who received instruction from God but had no Mediator, that one would not yield to the serpent? Is Christ's redeemed humanity so weak that unless Satan and his angels are destroyed, they would still be led into sin?

> *Many Christians have a weak understanding of what God's grace does.*

The "great salvation" which God has supplied saves completely. Hallelujah! Hallelujah! In that fearful time, God's people of faith demonstrate this truth, all to the glory of God.

God breaks His silence. With the seventh plague, "a loud voice comes out of the temple, from the throne, saying, "It is done" (Rev. 16:17)! "The Lord shall roar from on high, and utter His voice from His holy habitation...A noise shall come to the ends of the earth, for the Lord has a controversy with the nations. He enters into judgment with all flesh. He will give them that are wicked to the sword...The slain of the Lord shall be from one end of the earth to the other" (Jer. 25:30, 33; see Rev. 19:11–16, 20, 21).

Today, heaven is still speaking through the Bible and by the Holy Spirit. The disquiet and longing for something that people feel are the Holy Spirit awakening them to a new life. Heaven calls, "Come! Come! Read God's Word; something will happen." "Being born again... by the word of God which lives and abides forever"; "Of His own will He brought us forth with the word of truth" (1 Pet. 1:23; James 1:18). Come to Jesus now. "Today choose to hear His voice, harden not your heart" (Ps. 95:7; Heb. 4:7).

The Real Conspiracy

"A great sign appeared... and the dragon stood before the woman... so that when she gave birth he might devour her child. And she gave birth to a Son who is to rule all the nations with a rod of iron. And her child was caught up to God and His throne..."

Christ cried out, "It is finished," and died. At that moment, victory over sin and Satan was secured (Rev. 12:5, 10). Jesus Christ, the Lamb at the throne of God, controls the future.

"Now the salvation, and the power, and the kingdom of our God and the authority of His Christ have come, for the accuser of our brethren has been thrown down, who continually accuses them before our God." Satan accused Job before God (Job 1 and 2; Zech. 3:1). Satan lost any and all standing he may have had in heaven (see Rom. 3:26). "For this reason rejoice, O heavens and you who dwell in them. Woe to the earth because the devil has come down to you having great wrath, knowing he has only a short time." Satan now directs all of his conspiracy against the human race.

The dragon persecuted the woman who gave birth to the man-child, but God nourished her in the wilderness for a time, times, and half a time. The serpent poured water like a river out of his mouth that he might cause her to be swept away, but the earth helped the woman. The dragon was enraged with the woman and went to make war with the rest of her offspring who keep the commandments of God and hold to the testimony of Jesus (adapted from Rev. 12). **This is the unrecognized but real conspiracy that is in progress.**

"The serpent poured water like a river out of his mouth that he might cause the woman to be swept away." What does this tell us? We are reminded of the first appearance of the serpent. It was in Eden and out of his mouth came a flood of words that deceived the first woman. Centuries later, Satan used the mouth of the "little horn" of Daniel's prophecies to flood Christianity with words contrary to the truth of the Word which God has given. Revelation 16:13–14 tells us that out of the mouths of the dragon, beast, and false prophet come teachings supported by miracles to impose the false worship taught by the beast and his image. This is what has gathered the nations to war against Christ.

Satan has used many media to spread thousands of ideas that undermine and are in conflict with the Word of God. The world's culture is overflowing with them. They received prominence in the Enlightenment and Darwin's theories as the foundation for science, as well as in all the religions of the world. The popular conspiracy theories are more of Satan's strategy to keep people from knowing about the real conspiracy that he inflicts on the world. Self-centered human nature continues to voice more and more of the wisdom of the serpent. "When the Son of Man comes will He find faith on the earth?"

Another challenge that Bible prophecy poses to the current conspiracy theories is as follows: The theories say nothing about the papacy's involvement in world politics. It is the Jews who are the conspirators in the popular theories. If, as it is claimed, the Pope played a significant role in the collapse of the Soviet Union, then certainly the Roman Church must be involved in political intrigue.

Why did the Soviet Union collapse? The serpent's wisdom cannot provide what it promises. Self-centered human nature, supported by atheism, made it impossible for the goal of a classless utopia to be achieved. The economy controlled by the Kremlin stagnated. It could not sustain the cost it took to be a military superpower and keep the parts of the Soviet Union under control.

What about the one-world government? According to the Bible, there will not be one. God intervened at the Tower of Babel to prevent a one-world government (see Gen. 11:6–9).

Daniel 2:44—"in the days of these kings shall the God of heaven set up" His kingdom.

The Real Conspiracy

Rev. 16: 14—"the spirit of devils working miracles go to the kings of the earth to gather them to the war..."

The ten kings are deceived into uniting with the beast for a particular purpose. When it does not work according to the way it was sold to them, they turn on the beast (Rev. 17:12–17).

Consider the United Nations. It is thoroughly unable to exercise any compelling power. Consider the Afghan War. The U.S. and European nations, as well as Canada and Australia, agreed to the war and sent troops, but the troops did not combine under one command. The European Union was formed for economic purposes, yet the various nations maintain their independence. Nations will work together for a common purpose, but they will not unite into a single government. The working together of nations, religions, and businesses to support the mark of the beast for what is labeled *the common good* constitutes Babylon.

The Prophetic Beasts of Daniel 7, 8, and Revelation 13

The word "beast" is often used in the Bible. It usually references animals, but it is also used symbolically and prophetically. The first animal specifically named in the Bible is the serpent. The sheep is the second named animal. "The dragon of old, the serpent" and the Lamb are also the last two animals named in the Bible (Gen. 3:1; 4:2; Rev. 20:2; 22:1, 3). The word "cattle" (Gen. 1:24–26, KJ) is more of a generic term. That word is translated 150 times as "beast". Another Hebrew word is used in Genesis 4:20, which speaks of "the father of those who have cattle."

Prophetic Beasts

The four beasts of Daniel 7:3, 5, 6, 7, 11, and 12 are four kings or kingdoms (vs. 17, 23, 24). They parallel the four kingdoms of the great image of Daniel 2—Babylon, Media-Persia, Greece, and Rome. Daniel 8 presents a ram as Media-Persia and a male-goat as Greece (vs. 20, 21). Babylon is not mentioned because its rule was about to end.

In the prophecies of Daniel 7 and 8, it is the "little horn" that becomes "exceedingly great" that is the focus of the vision. It is "different." Its power and control come not from military might but by its "speaking." It claims to speak for God and is supported by the beast (political power) of which it is a part.

This horn represents a man who "speaks great things" and "great words" (Dan. 7: 8, 11, 20). He "makes war against the saints", "speaks great words against the Most High," "wears down the saints," "thinks to change time and laws," and "prevails for a time, times and half a time" (vs. 21, 25). Daniel 8:9–12 and 23–25 further describe the activities of the "horn" power. People are deceived into believing that it speaks as God and for God. This is why kings and nations used their power to support it and destroy its enemies.

Revelation 11:7 introduces "the beast from the abyss." This beast is not presented as a king or kingdom. It does not arise out of the sea or from the earth, but as an ideology that makes war against God's two witnesses [ancient writings depict a war between the gods and a dragon of chaos (abyss)]. They also refer to an evil seven-headed dragon (see *Seventh-day Adventist Bible Commentary*, vol. 4, on Isa. 27:1; vol. 8, p. 668, "Leviathan").

Revelation unmasks Satan's war against God, His truth, and people. It is not presenting a general world history. In His letters to the seven churches, Christ referred to Satan, his seat, synagogue, and deceptive work (2:9, 10, 13, 24; 3:9). It is Satan who is behind all these efforts to destroy the gospel and church. He has used individuals, governments, and other organizations to accomplish his goal.

The next prophetic beast presented is the seven-headed dragon of Revelation 12:3–9. This beast is identified as "the old serpent, the devil and Satan." This gives further understanding of the beast from the abyss. He began his war against God in heaven. Then he was able to establish it on earth. Satan lost his battle against the "Manchild," the promised Redeemer. Enraged, Satan carries on his war with increased intensity (vs. 13–17).

Mark of the Beast-2

What makes the Papacy and its head, the Pope, to be identified as the antichrist, little horn/beast power of Daniel 7, 8, and Revelation 13–20? It is the acts and the claims made by the Bishop of Rome. One can go back 1,000 years and discover this identification being made. As early as A.D. 604, Gregory the Great, Bishop of Rome, wrote to Emperor Mauricius Augustus, protesting the claim of the Patriarch of Constantinople to be called the Universal Priest. Gregory wrote, "Whoever calls himself, or desires to be called, Universal Priest, is in his elation the precursor of Antichrist, because he proudly puts himself above all others. Nor is it by dissimilar pride is he led into this error; for as that perverse one wishes to appear as God above all men, so whosoever this one is who covets being called sole priest, he extols himself above all others" [*Seventh-day Adventist Bible Students Source Book, Commentary Reference Series*, Vol. 9, p. 36, Item 58 (reference gives original source)].

How is it that the title so strongly opposed by the Bishop of Rome as an antichrist title has come to be proudly assumed by his successors? Gregory's identification and judgment stand.

Jesus made it clear that His "going" was not leaving his disciples as orphans, having no leadership. By his going to be with the Father, He would send to them a more powerful Helper than He had been to them here on earth. His ministry in heaven would be entirely devoted to enabling them to take the gospel to all the earth (see John 14:12–20).

The "other Helper" that Jesus promised is the Holy Spirit, "whom the Father will send in My name (John 14:16–18, 26). This makes Him the Vicar of Christ. "He will teach you all things, and bring to your remembrance all things that I said to you" (John 15:26; 16:6–15; Luke 24:46–49; Acts 1:1–5, 8; 2). No human could ever be Christ's vicar. The Apostle Peter never claimed that he had been appointed the head of the apostles and church, nor did he ever receive such a recognition during his life (1 Peter 5:1, 4).

The New Testament declares that Christ is the foundation, the builder, and head of His church (Matt. 16:18; 1 Cor. 3:11; Eph. 1:20–22; 5:23; Col. 1:18; 2:19). It also tells us that from out of the Christian community would arise people who would lead others to follow them and their teachings (Matt. 7:15; 24:5, 11, 24; 2 Cor. 11:13–15; 2 Thess. 2:3–10; 2 Peter 2:1, 2; 1 John 2:18, 19). Revelation depicts that all through Christian history Satan has warred against Christ and the gospel. He infiltrates Christianity to use it for his purposes.

Revelation 13 pictures his final effort, but Christ will have His faithful remnant (Rev. 12:17; 14:12; 20:4–6; 21 and 22). They worship God according to His commandments, not as the Papacy and world command.

Following are Claims Made by and for the Pope

It took centuries for the Imperial Papacy to develop. There was severe competition between the Bishop of Rome and the Patriarch of Constantinople as to who was the greatest. Though the Code of Justinian recognized the Roman pope's headship over all the churches, it took years for it to be actualized (*Source Book*, Items, #1134, #1135).

The following are from the *Seventh-day Adventist Bible Students Source Book*, where the complete source reference is given—pages 675–707, numbers 1113–1171:

#1120—Bishop of Rome is Peter's Successor. Letter of Jerome to the Bishop of Rome. "This I know is the rock on which the Church is built. This is the house where alone the pascal lamb can be rightly eaten. This is the Ark of Noah and he who is not in it shall perish when the flood prevails."

#1121—Oration at Fifth Lateran Council. "For thou are the shepherd, thou art the physician. thou art the director, thou art the husbandman; finally thou art another God on earth."

Mark of the Beast–2

#1122—"For the pope alone is said to be the Vicar of God; wherefore only what is bound or loosed by him is held to be bound or loosed by God Himself. no appeal holds when it is made from the pope to God because there is one consistory of the pope himself and of God himself."

#1123—"The pope is of such great authority and power that he can modify, explain, or even interpret divine laws." "The pope can modify divine law, since his power is not of man, but of God, and he acts in place of God upon earth, with the fullest power of binding and loosing his sheep."

#1124—"We define that the Holy Apostolic See and the Roman Pontiff holds the primacy over the whole world, and that the Roman Pontiff himself is the successor of the blessed Peter, prince of the apostle s, and the true vicar of Christ, the head of the whole church, and the father and doctor of all Christians; and that to him was given by our Lord Jesus Christ, full power to feed, rule, and govern the universal church."

#1125—"The pope is crowned with a triple crown, as king of heaven, and of earth, and of the lower regions."

#1132—Claim of Leo XIII. "We hold upon this earth the place of God Almighty."

#1128—Pope Gregory VII, (Dictates of Hildebrand) "I. The Roman Church was founded by the Lord alone. 2. That the Roman Pontiff alone is justly called universal. 3. That he alone can depose bishops or restore them. 9. That all princes should kiss the feet of the pope alone. 12. That it is lawful for him to depose emperors... 18. That his sentence ought not to be reviewed by anyone; and he alone can review the decisions of all. 19. That he ought to be judged by no one. 22. That the Roman Church never erred; nor will it according to Scripture ever err. 27. That he alone can absolve subjects from their allegiance to unrighteous rulers."

#1129—Every human creature is subject to the pope, Boniface VIII. In the Bull, Unam Sanctam. "That there is one Holy Catholic and Apostolic Church. We are impelled by our faith to believe and to hold-this we do firmly believe and openly confess–and outside of this there is neither salvation or remission of sins," (closing sentence) "We moreover, proclaim, declare, and pronounce that it is altogether necessary to salvation to every human being to be subject to the Roman Pontiff."

The Gospel and the Catechism of the Catholic Church

"JOHN PAUL, BISHOP SERVANT OF THE SERVANTS OF GOD FOR EVERLASTING MEMORY, To my Venerable Brothers the Cardinals, Patriarchs, Archbishops, Priests, Deacons, and all the People of God.

"GUARDING THE DEPOSIT OF FAITH IS THE MISSION WHICH THE LORD ENTRUSTED TO HIS CHURCH, and which she fulfills in every age. The Second Vatican Ecumenical Council, which was opened 30 years ago by my predecessor Pope John XXIII, of happy memory, had as its intention and purpose to highlight the Church's apostolic and pastoral mission and by making the truth of the Gospel shine forth to lead all people to seek and receive Christ's love which surpasses all knowledge" (p. 1).

This is how John Paul II began his introduction and presentation of this Catechism. He tells how it was prepared and closes with the following words.

"The Doctrinal Value of the Text. The Catechism of the Catholic Church, which I approved June 25th last and the publication of which I today order by virtue of my Apostolic Authority, is a statement of the Church's faith and of catholic doctrine, attested to or illumined by Sacred Scripture, the Apostolic Tradition, and the Church's Magisterium. I declare it to be the norm for teaching the faith and thus a valid and legitimate instrument for ecclesial communion" (p. 5).

"The approval and publication of the Catechism of the catholic Church represents a service which the Successor of Peter wishes to offer to the Holy Catholic Church, to all the particular Churches in peace and communion with the Apostolic See: the service, that is, of supporting and confirming the faith of all the Lord Jesus' disciples (Lk. 22:32), as well as strengthening the bonds of unity in the same Apostolic faith...

"This catechism is given to them that it may be a sure and authentic reference for teaching catholic doctrine and particularly for preparing local catechisms. It is meant to support ecumenical efforts that are moved by the holy desire for the unity of all Christians, showing carefully the content and wondrous harmony of the catholic faith. The Catechism of the Catholic Church, lastly, is offered to every individual who asks us to give an account of the hope that is in us (cf. 1 Pet. 3:15) and who wants to know what the Catholic Church believes" (p. 6).

"At the conclusion of this document presenting the Catechism of the Catholic Church, I beseech the Blessed Virgin Mary, Mother of the incarnate Word and Mother of the Church to support with her powerful intercession the catechetical work of the entire Church on every level, at this time when she is called to a new effort of evangelization. May the light of the true faith free humanity from the ignorance and slavery of sin in order to lead it to the only freedom worthy of the name (cf. John 8:32): that of life in Jesus Christ under the guidance of the Holy Spirit.

"Given October 11, 1992, the thirtieth anniversary of the opening of the Second Vatican Ecumenical Council, in the fourteenth year of my Pontificate." John Paul II. signed his name (pp. 6, 7).

Did Christ appoint a human organization to be the infallible teacher of His Church? No. "I will not leave you orphans. I will come to you." "The Father will give you another Advocate. He will abide with you forever...The Comforter who is the Holy Spirit, who the Father will send in My Name, He shall teach you all things, and bring all things to your remembrance, whatever I have said to you." "I have many things to say to you but you cannot bear them now. When He, the Spirit of truth is come, He will guide you into all truth. He shall show you things to come. He shall glorify Me for he shall receive of mine and shall show it to you" (John 14:16, 26; 16:12–14; Acts 17:10, 11).

Christ, the Holy Spirit, and the Bible are the supreme authority for the church. Believers cannot make new truth or change God's truth. All any believer or church can do is witness to what God has done through our Lord Jesus Christ.

(1) Speaking, for God and as God, is claimed for the Roman Catholic Church.

The following quotations are from the: COMPLETE AND UPDATED CATECHISM OF THE CATHOLIC CHURCH, with presentation by John Paul II, given October 11, 1992.

The Magisterium of the Church.

85 "The task of giving an authentic interpretation of the Word of God, whether in written form, or in the form of Tradition, has been entrusted to the living, teaching office of the Church alone. Its authority in this matter is exercised in the name of Jesus Christ." this means that the task of interpretation has been entrusted to the bishops in communion with the successor of Peter, the Bishop of Rome" (p. 32).

> *Christ, the Holy Spirit, and the Bible are the supreme authority for the church. Believers cannot make new truth or change God's truth.*

87 "Mindful of Christ's words to his apostles: 'He who hears you hears me,' the faithful receive with docility the teachings and directives that their pastors give them in different forms" (p. 33).

95 "It is clear therefore that in the supremely wise arrangement of God, sacred Tradition, Sacred Scripture, and the Magisterium of the Church are so connected and associated that one of them cannot stand without the others. Working together, each in its own way, under the action of the one Holy Spirit, they all contribute effectively to the salvation of souls" (p. 34).

(This says that Scripture cannot stand on its own. The Bible is made secondary to church teaching).

100 "The task of interpreting the Word of God authentically has been entrusted solely to the Magisterium of the Church, that is to the Pope and to the bishops in communion with him" (p. 35).

890 "The mission of the Magisterium is linked to the definitive nature of the covenant established by God with his people in Christ. It is this Magisterium's task to preserve God's people from deviations and defections and to guarantee them the objective

Mark of the Beast–2

possibility of professing the true faith without error. Thus, the pastoral duty of the Magisterium is aimed at seeing to it that the People of God abides in the truth that liberates. To fulfill this service, Christ endowed the Church's shepherds with the charism of infallibility in matters of faith and morals. The exercise of this charism takes several forms" (p. 256; see also #891).

894 "The bishops as vicars and legates of Christ, govern the particular Churches assigned to them by their counsels, exhortations, and example, but over and above that also by the authority and sacred power which indeed they ought to exercise so as to edify, in the spirit of service which is that of their Master" (p. 257).

The Mormon Church also claims that without the priesthood as is restored to them, one cannot know or have the gospel (see *The Restoration of the Gospel of Jesus Christ*, pp. 8–11).

A Further Understanding of Babylon in Revelation

(from the Book of Daniel)

The priests of Babylon regarded their city as the "navel" of the earth and the "gate of God." Jerusalem, with its temple and claim that "God placed His name there" and made His will known to His people (Ex. 25:22), was seen as a rival by Babylon.

"Nebuchadnezzar king of Babylon came to Jerusalem and besieged it. And the Lord gave Jehoiakim king of Judah into his hand along with some of the vessels of the of the house of God; and he brought them unto the land of Shinar, to the house of his gods" (Dan. 1:1, 2; also Jer. 27:19–22).

"The fact that these vessels, as well as the house of the pagan god are mentioned twice, and this detail is given at the very outset of the narrative indicates the significance of this action. Although it was a common practice and may be seen as a perfectly normal procedure, we do not have an incidental or irrelevant beginning. On the contrary, it is the theme of the book and the key to everything that follows.

"This assessment is not difficult to follow. The book of Daniel deals indeed with the issues of superiority and defeat, of usurpation and worship. Therefore it is not accidental that the removal of the temple vessels sets the stage as it were, for the theme that is treated in the rest of the book.

"It becomes clear from the context in Daniel 1:1,2, and from ancient Near-Eastern understanding of temple worship that the act of removing the articles from the Jerusalem temple and placing them in a pagan shrine was viewed as a great victory for the conquering party." Winfried Vogel, "Cultic Motifs and Themes in the Book of Daniel" (*Journal of The Adventist Theological Society*, Spring 1996, pp. 27, 28).

Belshazzar's pride led him to defy God, and the vessels from God's temple have a prominent part in Belshazzar's feast and the fall of Babylon (see Dan. 5:2–4, 22, 23). In Revelation, Babylon is "seated on many waters". Nations support her. She has a "golden cup in her hand." She thinks, "I sit a queen and am not a widow. I will never know mourning" (Rev. 17:1, 4; 18:7). What Babylon does is take the "vessels" of God and then serve its own "wine" in them.

As a false teacher, Babylon clothes herself as a Christian (see Rev. 14:8; 17:2; 18:3). Babylon corrupts the gospel and worship of God. "Woe to you... for you are like whitewashed tombs which on the outside appear beautiful, but inside they are full of dead men's bones and lawlessness. Even so you too outwardly appear righteous to men, but inwardly you are full of hypocrisy and lawlessness" (Matt. 7:15; 23:27, 28).

John Paul II placed the new *Catechism of The Catholic Church* in the Deposit of the Faith on October 11, 1992.

In reading it, one observes a focus that is different from the teaching of the gospel as it is given to us in the New Testament. In the New Testament, human salvation is Christ-centered. In the Catechism, it is Catholic Church- and priest-centered. The apostles taught us to put our faith in what God has done through Jesus Christ. The Catechism teaches that one must depend on the activity of priests to receive salvation.

The Abomination of Desolation (Matthew 24:15; Mark 13:14)

What is it?

In the Bible, the word "abomination" refers to false practices of worship. They were practices that were common in the countries surrounding Israel but specifically prohibited by God. In Leviticus 18:20–30, the word "abomination" is used five times. It defiles people and land. Particular abominations were not just practiced by the people, but also incorporated into their worship (see Deut. 18:9–12; 2 Kings 21:1–14; 23:13, 24; Jeremiah 2:7, 8; 6:15; 7:9, 10, 29–32; 32:28–35).

"I brought you into the fruitful land… but you came and defiled my land, and made My inheritance an abomination… and the prophets prophesied by Baal." Jer. 2:7,8

"Will you steal, murder, and commit adultery, swear falsely, and offer sacrifice to Baal, and walk after other gods that you have not known, then come and stand before me in this house which is called by My name and say, 'we are delivered' to do all these abominations. Has this house which is called by My name become a den of robbers?... For the sons of Judah have done that which is evil in My sight declares the Lord, they have set their abominations in the house which is called by My name to defile it" (Jer. 7:9–11, 30).

"I taught them…but they put their abominations in the house which is called by My name to defile it. And they built the high places of Baal...that they should do this abomination to cause Judah to sin" (Jer. 32:33–35).

The temple, with its services, was to be a constant reminder of the awfulness of sin. Sin causes death. At the same time, the temple taught that God was among them with His great, generous acts for their salvation. For the people, their service was to be an expression of their need for and faith in God's provision for them.

In 2 Kings 21:1–12, we find an account of what Manasseh did in promoting false worship. Verse 11 speaks of all these "abominations". In 2 Kings 23:4–13 and 24, we find the abominations that had come into the worship of the Jews. King Josiah, in his revival, stopped the abominable practices in the temple. His sons returned to them (see 23:31, 32, 36, 37).

False teachings and practices were brought into God's true worship. False teachings and practices replaced God's true worship. Their changed worship allowed them to keep their pride and lust, rather than make them a holy people. These "abominations" brought calamity and desolation to Judah and Jerusalem. Daniel, in his prayer, spoke of the "desolations" that had come to his people (9:2, 17, 18).

"I will ruin, ruin, ruin" (Ezekiel 21:27). Three times the armies of Babylon came and captured the city. The first time, people were taken to Babylon. The second time, more people were exiled, and all wealth was taken. The third time, the walls were broken down, and the city burned.

What caused the capture and desolation of Jerusalem? Before Babylonian armies came and captured the city, Babylonian ideas and practices had captured the lives of the people and were made part of their beliefs and worship. Before the armies desolated the city, false beliefs desolated the character of the people (see Jer. 25:2–7).

They went after other gods (v. 6). They rebelled against the word of God which was spoken by their prophets. Here we see what the "abomination of desolation" is and how it works. The abomination is false worship practiced and required by those who claim to represent God. The desolation is the harvest of such rebellion.

The Abomination of Desolation (Matthew 24:15; Mark 13:14)

Though Daniel lived through the time that desolation came to Jerusalem, he prophesied of an abomination of desolation still in the future (see 8:13; 9:26, 27; 11:31; 12:11).

Jesus referred to Daniel's prophecy (see Matt. 24:15; Mark 13:14). It was Daniel 9:26–27 that was fulfilled in the destruction of Jerusalem in A.D. 70. That, and what occurred in A.D. 135, was because of their rejection of the Messiah. More would yet transpire. When Jesus spoke of the necessity of worshipping in spirit and truth (John 4:23, 24), He was teaching His followers that they must not bring into their worship of Him the ideas and practices of other beliefs. After Constantine combined church and state to promote Roman Christianity, many pagan symbols and practices were "Christianized" and brought into the fold.

Revelation 17:4–5 depicts the harlot Babylon as she holds her golden cup full of abominations, which she passes off as the "water of life." She has changed the glorious gospel that brings life into a religious system that brings desolation and death (see Rev. 6:7, 8; Prov. 16:25).

The abomination of desolation unfolds because Christianity replaces the clear teaching of the Bible with human ideas and practices. Christianity is used to promote world unity and political goals rather than bring people to salvation in Jesus Christ and prepare them for His soon coming.

The apostasy of Christian Rome established the "little horn". The glorious, life-giving gospel depicted under the first seal of Revelation was changed and threatened death to those who refused to conform to its teachings (fourth seal, Rev. 6:7, 8).

The final apostasy, "the third woe", is pictured in Revelation 13:12–17. Such a rejection of God, His truth, and final appeal of 14:6–12 and 18:1–4 brings its harvest of the seven last plagues. The earth will lie in desolation

In the beginning, God created the beautiful, living earth, as a home for humans made in His image. Accepting and enforcing the deceptive teachings of Satan results in desolation and destruction on earth. Isaiah 14:16–20 says this about Satan: "Those who see you will gaze at you. They will consider you, saying, 'Is this the man who made the earth to tremble, who shook kingdoms, who made the earth like a wilderness, and overthrew its cities? You ruined your country, you have slain your people." False, rebellious teachings result in the desolation of the earth (see Isa. 24:1–6).

E.G. White's *The Great Controversy*, in its comments about the destruction of Jerusalem in A.D. 70, refers to Christ's words in Matthew 24:15–18: "Therefore when you see the abomination of desolation spoken of by Daniel the prophet standing in the holy place...then let those who are in Judea flee to the mountains" (pp. 26, 45). The first thing Christ's words tell us is that Antiochus IV was not the fulfillment of Daniel's prophecy which, according to Jesus, was then still future. The city of Jerusalem and some distance beyond it walls were regarded as holy ground. When the idolatrous standards of Rome were set up, that was seen as the sign, so when the Roman army temporarily withdrew, believers in Christ fled from the area.

"When the idolatrous standards of the Romans should be set up in holy ground, then..." Suppose we change the sentence to read, "When the idolatrous standards of Babylon are set up in Christianity and enforced, then we know the War of Armageddon is about to end." Flee to Christ. Take refuge in Him and the promises of His Word. "I will say of the Lord, He is my refuge and my fortress: my God, in Him will I trust" (Ps. 91:2).

The Lord's Supper

The accounts in Matthew 26:26–30, Mark 14:22–25, Luke 22:18–20, and 1 Corinthians 11:23–25 tell us that Jesus took bread, blessed it, and then gave it to the disciples. Then He took the cup and did the same. He said that it was a new covenant in His blood. The bread was His body—the perfect life He lived for us is by His death given to us. The cup was His blood shed for us. His new, better covenant was ratified, not by the blood of an animal, but with His blood (see Heb. 8:6–8, 13; 9:8–15).

Jesus said, "Do this in remembrance of Me." The Greek word for "remembrance" here means "to remember again". God instructed Israel to "remember" the mighty works of God in delivering them from Egypt and making them His covenant people (see Ex. 13:3; Deut. 5:1–15). How much more are we to remember the great acts of God in Christ that provide for our deliverance from sin and eternal salvation.

Paul, in giving the instruction he had received from the Lord, wrote, "For as often as you eat this bread, and drink this cup, you do declare [or preach] the Lord's death until He comes" (1 Cor. 11:23, 26).

The communion service unites the present—"as often as you eat this bread and drink this cup"—the past—"the Lord's death"—and the future—"till he comes." Christ instituted this great memorial service for His followers. It is the visible reminder of the great salvation and hope that He has given to us by His death.

"For Christ also has once suffered for sins, the righteous for the unrighteous, that He might bring us to God, being put to death in the flesh, but made alive by the Spirit" (1 Peter 3:18). Jesus has become the one, eternal Melchizedekian High Priest. He can save completely those who come to God by Him, seeing He ever lives to make intercession for them (Heb. 7:14–28). Unlike other high priests He does not need to offer sacrifices day after day, first for His own sins, and then for the sins of the people. He needed no sacrifice for Himself. He was the Lamb which God supplied to bear away the sins of the world. His sacrifice was not by the blood of goats and calves, but by His own blood, ONCE for all (Heb. 9:11,12, 25-28; 10:10). "Not by the blood of goats and calves, but by His own blood he entered in ONCE into the holy place having obtained eternal redemption for us." "By that will [His decision] we are sanctified through the offering of the body of Jesus ONCE for all" (9:12; 10:10).

> *The communion service unites the present—"as often as you eat this bread and drink this cup"—the past—"the Lord's death"—and the future—"till he comes."*

The sufficiency of Christ's "once for all", sacrificial death was prefigured during Israel's sojourn in the wilderness. To bring lifegiving water to Israel in the wilderness, the rock was to be smitten, but only once. The second time that water was needed, Moses was not to strike the rock, but in faith to speak to it. His striking it again kept him out of Canaan (see 1 Cor. 10:4; Ex. 17:6; Num. 20:8, 10, 11).

From Acts to Revelation, Christ is praised for the great, marvelous, and wonderful salvation He has provided by His sacrifice on the cross. He is the one Mediator (see 1 Tim. 2:5). All that God has provided comes to us individually as we put our faith in Christ.

The Emphasis of the New Testament

Jesus, His sacrifice, which provided salvation for humanity, and His second advent are the main themes of the New Testament.

Matthew 26:28—"My blood of the new covenant" (see also Mark 14:24; Luke 22:20).

Acts 20:20—"The church which He has purchased with His own blood."

Romans 3:25—"through faith in His blood."

Romans 5:9—"Being justified by His blood."

1 Corinthians 10:16—"a sharing in the blood and body of Christ."

1 Corinthians 11:25,26—"This cup is the new covenant in My blood, you drink it in remembrance of Me. For as often as you eat this bread and drink this cup, you proclaim the Lord's death until He comes."

Ephesians 1:7—"We have redemption through His blood."

Ephesians 2:13—Gentiles, who were far away, "are brought near by the blood of Christ."

Colossians 1:14—"We have redemption through His blood."

Colossians 1:20—Reconciled all things, "having made peace by the blood of His cross."

Hebrews 9:7—Only once a year could the Aaronic high priest enter the most holy place, and that required blood.

Hebrews 9:12, 14—"But when Christ appeared as High Priest of good things to come, through His own blood he entered the Holy place, once for all, having obtained eternal redemption

Armageddon's Glorious End

for us." "How much more will the blood of Christ...cleanse your conscience from dead works to serve the living God."

Hebrews 10:19—We can "enter the holy place by the blood of Jesus."

Hebrews 12:22, 24—Christian faith is centered in Christ, "the city of the living God, the heavenly Jerusalem," His "sprinkled blood."

Hebrews 13:12—"Jesus, that He might sanctify the people through His own blood..."

Hebrews 13:20—What God does for us, is through the blood of the eternal covenant.

1 Peter 1:2—"the foreknowledge (plan) of God, the sanctifying work of the Spirit, that you may obey Jesus being sprinkled with His blood."

1 Peter 1:18, 19—Our redemption was not of gold, silver, or material things, "but with the precious blood of Christ."

1 John 1:7—"and the blood of Jesus His Son cleanses us from all sin."

1 John 5:5–8—Jesus, the Son of God, came by water and blood. The Spirit, the water, and the blood all agree. Jesus was fully human. There is no dualism in the gospel.

Revelation 1:7—"He washed us from our sins in His own blood...."

Revelation 5:9—"You did purchase for God with Your own blood, people from every tribe, language and nation."

Revelation 7:14—"They have washed their robes and made them white in the blood of the Lamb."

Revelation 12:11—"They overcame him because of the blood of the Lamb..." (see also Eph. 5:2; Heb. 9:26; 10:7, 12).

There is no focus on establishing some earthly city or Christian kingdom. "Looking for the blessed hope and the glorious appearing of our great God and Savior, Jesus Christ" (Titus 2:13).

Messiah, and the Israel of God

It was the Monday or Tuesday of the week in which Jesus was arrested and put to death. He had been teaching in the temple. He knew the time had come when He would be delivered up. How he longed for the salvation of the Jewish people! He gave lesson after lesson to open their hearts that they might say "yes" to Him (see Matt. 21–23; Luke 20–22).

There were Scribes and Pharisees that were drawn to Him. Jesus worked to save them even more than the common people. They were leaders. They could greatly influence the people to receive Him. However, most of them were doing the opposite. They listened to Him to get words they could use to condemn Him and put Him to death.

Now Jesus, as a faithful prophet, spoke warnings and woes on the leaders of the people (see Matt. 23). The woes which He declared were only those which they were bringing upon themselves. They were woes of which the nation had been warned from its beginning.

Centuries before, as God was bringing Israel from Egypt into Canaan, He had given them an impressive ceremony. The Lord chose two mountains—Mount Ebal and Mount Gerizim. One was the mount of blessing and the other the mount of cursing. The account is found in Deuteronomy 11:26–32 and chapters 27 and 28. Six tribes were to stand on Mount Gerizim and the other six on Mount Ebal. Those on Mount Gerizim were to speak of the blessings that would be theirs if they faithfully obeyed God.

Those on Mount Ebal spoke of the curses that would result if they disobeyed God's laws. If they disobeyed, nations would come against them and take them captive. They would be scattered among all people from one end of the earth to the other.

Israel's leaders understood this. Centuries later, Solomon, in his dedicatory prayer for the great temple he built for God, referred to these very things (see 2 Chron. 6:10–42).

Jeremiah, addressing Judah and Jerusalem, forcefully reminded them that they had violated God's covenant (see 11:1–17). He reminded the nation that their standing in God's plan was conditional on their faithfulness to Him (see 18:5–12). Just as Adam and Eve could only remain in the Garden of Eden if they were faithful to God, so the nation of Israel could serve as God's chosen nation only as they remained faithful to Him.

God's prophets from Moses onward had all repeated this theme. Because of forsaking God, the nation had often been oppressed. Israel had gone into captivity once. The city and temple had been destroyed by Babylon. They had returned as had been promised by God. Now the 490 years spoken of by Daniel were in the final "week". "Messiah the prince" was among His people (see Dan. 9:24, 25). "The owner of the vineyard" (God, the owner of Israel) had sent His Son (see Matt. 21:33–45).

The 490 years that had been appointed for the Jews and Jerusalem were ending. "Seventy weeks have been decreed for your people and your holy city" (Dan. 9:24). Would the nation fulfill God's plan for them, or would they reject their Messiah?

Their stubbornness and rebellion filled Christ with grief. On that Palm Sunday, as He approached Jerusalem and viewed the city, He wept over it, saying, "If you had known in this your day the things that belong to your peace, but now they are hidden from your eyes...you did not recognize the time of your visitation" (Luke 19:44). In sending His Son, God visited His people.

"He came to His own, and His own people received Him not" (John 1:11). "Therefore I say to you, 'The kingdom of God will be taken away from you and given to a nation producing the fruit of it'" (Matt. 21:43). This has come to pass. It is Christ's people of faith that receive the promises and constitute the kingdom of God.

Messiah, and the Israel of God

Before we look at what Paul and Peter wrote in the N.T., we should remember that their background as Jews gave them strong prejudices in favor of the Jewish nation and against Gentiles as not being acceptable to God. Paul especially grew up nurtured in the glories of his Jewish heritage. Reaching his adult years, "He excelled others in advancing in Judaism, being more extremely zealous for my ancestral traditions." Paul was "a Pharisee and a son of Pharisees", taught by the famous Gamaliel and "a Hebrew of the Hebrews, as to the law a Pharisee and blameless" (Gal. 1:13, 14; Acts 22:3; 26:5; Phil 3:4, 5).

As a Jew, Paul dedicated himself to destroy the followers of Jesus (see Acts 9:1, 2; 22:4; 26:11). Then Jesus revealed Himself to Paul as the One he was persecuting, and his life was turned upside down and inside out. He surrendered to Jesus in a commitment from which he never wavered.

In Jesus Christ, Paul began to see his nation, religion, and Jewish life and history in a new way. It was the way that God had always intended it to be understood. The "seed of David", God's promised Messiah, had appeared, inaugurating the kingdom of heaven (see Matt. 4:17; 10:7; Matt. 5–7). The "kingdom of heaven", proclaimed by Christ, was not a geographical area. It was His called-out people—people from every nation, Jew or Gentile, who in faith gave themselves to Him. They constitute His kingdom in this present age.

The New Testament church came under serious threat from Jews who accepted Jesus as the Messiah but insisted on circumcision, separation from Gentiles, and the practices which Jewish tradition had added. They refused to see the end of that which was abolished when Christ died, and the veil of the temple was ripped in two from top to bottom. They put the "new wine in old bottles" (Matt. 9:17; 2 Cor. 3:7–14).

That such believers were a serious threat to the gospel is evident by the arguments against them in several of the N.T. letters. Paul had been more diligent in those practices than most Jews, but it became apparent to him that becoming a Jew and conforming to those practices was not God's requirement.

Who is it that God considers as Jews—His special people? The answer can be found in 1 Pet. 2:9–10. Revelation 2:9 and 3:9 speak

Armageddon's Glorious End

of those who "say they are Jews and are not..." What do we find in Romans 2:28, 29? "For he is not a Jew who is one outwardly, neither is circumcision that which is outward in the flesh, but he is a Jew who is one inwardly; and circumcision is that which is of the heart, by the Spirit, not by the letter."

Paul further warns in Philippians 3:2, 3: "Beware of the false circumcision; for we are the true circumcision who worship in the Spirit of God, and glory in Christ Jesus, and put no confidence in the flesh" (NASB). "Even us whom He also called, not from among the Jews only, but also from among Gentiles. As He says also in Hosea, 'I will call those who were not My people, "My people"'" (Rom. 9:24–26, NASB; see also Eph. 2:11–22); Gentiles and Jews become "one new man, one body, a holy temple in Christ."

John the Baptist told the people not to think that because they were descendants of Abraham, they had any standing with God to the exclusion of all other people. "God could from stones raise up children to Abraham" (Matt. 3:9). Jesus repeated the same thought in John 8:39. It is faithfulness to God that renders one a descendant of Abraham. Nicodemus, a ruler of the Jews, was told by Jesus that unless he was "born of water and the Spirit" or "born again", he could neither "see" or "enter" the kingdom of God (John 3:3, 5). Being Jewish is not what gives one standing with God. Whether one is Jew or Greek, nationality is not what counts. "If you are Christ's, then are you Abraham's seed and heirs according to the promise" (Gal. 3:26, 28, 29). This fulfills God's covenant promise to Abraham that through his seed all the nations of the earth would be blessed" (Gen. 12:3; Gal. 3:6–8, 16–18).

"Israel" was not given by God to be an ethnic name. It was bestowed by God in recognition of Jacob's faith. Jacob would not let go. It was his prevailing, victorious faith in God's word that resulted in the name "Israel" (see Gen. 32:9–12, 24–30; Hosea 12:4; 1 John 5:4). By calling Jews "Israel", God was reminding them that He called them to be His servant, people of faith, and witness to the nations (see Isa. 44:21; 49:3, 6, 7).

It is from the words Christ spoke to Nicodemus, Romans 2:29 and 9:24–26, and Colossians 3:2–3 that we get "spiritual Israel" and "born of the Spirit." In God's sight, one is a Jew "by the Spirit,

Messiah, and the Israel of God

not by birth." Samaritan or Jew, true worshippers worship God in spirit (see John 4:23, 24). Paul, "the Pharisee of the Pharisees", could not boast of his Jewishness. His only boast and hope were in the cross of Christ. "Circumcision is nothing. Uncircumcision is nothing. A new creation is everything." Those who walk by this rule have received God's peace and mercy. They are the Israel of God (see Gal. 6:14–16).

There is an interesting historical note that fits into Revelation 2:8–9. It is mentioned in the book *God Cares*, vol. 2, p. 102. It is in reference to the persecution of Christians in the city of Smyrna. Polycarp was taken to the arena. He was told to deny Christ and save his life. He refused. The lions were full of human food, and it was past time for them to be used, so the crowd, especially Jews, cried for him to be burned. Though it was the Sabbath, the Jews, who were present, helped to gather brush and wood for the fire [Jews were prohibited such activity on the Sabbath (Num. 15:32–36)]. How fitting are Christ's words: "the blasphemy of those who say they are Jews but are not."

New Testament believers came to understand that literal Israel was replaced by the Christian Church. Christian history reveals that this became a widely held belief. Irenaeus, in *Against Heresies* (A.D. 177–195), book 5, chap. 33, sec. 3, pp. 562–563, interpreted Israel as the Christian church, the spiritual seed of Abraham (From, *Prophetic Faith of Our Fathers*, vol. I, p. 251). Without this understanding, Augustine could not have written *City of God*, in which he said that the promises made to the Jews were being realized in the established Christian Church.

The belief that focuses on Palestine, the Jews, and Jerusalem is the product of the futuristic view of prophecy that was promoted during the "Counter Reformation." The ideas coalesced in the early 1800s and were endorsed by Darby and Scofield in *The Scofield Reference Bible*. When the Second Assembly of the World Council of Churches met in Evanston, Illinois in the 1950s, and again in 1971 at the Jerusalem Conference on Bible Prophecy, there were scholars that presented the view that Israel was replaced by the Christian Church, and also those who promoted the view that ethnic Israel is the focus of Bible prophecy.

Armageddon's Glorious End

In the light of what Jesus said to His nation—"The kingdom of God is taken from you and given to a nation bringing forth the fruit thereof"—and the further teaching found in the New Testament, it is clear that Christ's words have come to pass. The Apostle Peter took the words spoken to Israel when they stood before Mt. Sinai (see Ex. 19:5, 6) and applied them to Christians: "You are built up a spiritual house... a chosen race, a royal priesthood, a holy nation, a people for God's own possession, for you were once not a people, but now you are the people of God" (1 Peter 2:5–10) (Jews no longer exist as twelve tribes). The saved from all nations enter New Jerusalem through twelve gates. The names of the twelve tribes on the gates identify them as the Israel of God. On the foundation of New Jerusalem are inscribed the names of the twelve apostles, not the names of Abraham, Isaac, and Jacob. The foundation which the apostles proclaimed was Jesus, and "no other foundation could be laid than the man Christ Jesus" (Rev. 21:12–14; Eph. 2:20; 1 Cor. 3:11).

The Apostle Paul was brought to understand that the Old Testament prophecies regarding Israel apply to the Christian Church. The true Israel, to whom belong the covenants and promises, is not the nation descended literally from Abraham, but the seed of Abraham by faith, both Jewish and Gentile Christians alike (see Rom. 4:13; 9:4, 6–8; 2:28, 29; 11:16; Gal. 3:16–29).

"I will be their God and they shall be My people" (2 Cor. 6:16–18). Paul uses the covenant language of the Old Testament and applies it to Christians (see Ezek. 11:20; 36:28; Jer. 7:23; 11:4; 30:22). Jesus is the "True Vine" (John 15:1–7) and "True Olive Tree" (Rom. 11).

Christ is the "Root" (Rom. 11:16–24). He gives life to and nourishes the branches. Believers, whether Jews or Gentiles, can only be branches on the tree. Branches that do not "abide in Him" are useless and will be burned. Any standing one has with God depends entirely upon faith in Christ as Lord and Savior. People of Hebrew heritage stand before God on the same basis as any other human does.

The New Testament gives no prophetic focus to the land of Palestine. Christ said locations in Palestine would cease to have distinct significance (see John 4:19–23). "Jerusalem which is above is our mother." Believers "come to Mount Zion, the city of the living God, the heavenly Jerusalem" (Gal. 4:26; Heb. 12:22). Isaiah had foretold that the Lord would create a new heaven and earth which would include the creation of a new Jerusalem. The Lord also said His servants would be called by another name (see Isa. 65:17, 18, 15). The "disciples were first called Christians at Antioch" (Acts 11:26). Messiah, God's Servant and Faithful Witness, by the life He lived, gave the witness that Israel had been called to give. By His suffering and death, He did what only God could accomplish, the redemption of His creation. It is from Jesus that we get the name "Christians".

It is troubling that so much attention is given to the Jews in Palestine while our risen Lord, ascended to the throne of God, is ignored. The building of a temple in Jerusalem is considered more relevant. Christ and His closing work on earth are overlooked. Jesus is at the throne of God "for us." It is His heavenly ministry for His church that is all important.

The Pentecost (see Acts 2) was the beginning of what Christ's heavenly ministry means for the world. On that day, Peter said, "He has sent forth this what you see and hear." Jesus had told them, "because I live, you will live also." We Christians are dependent upon Him and His heavenly ministry for access to God, the Holy Spirit, our witness, and success. He, the "Head of the church", "walks in the midst of His church, holding its ministers in His right hand" (Rev. 1:20). Through Him come the gifts which the Holy Spirit brings to the church. "He ever lives to make intercession for us." Because of Him, "This gospel of the kingdom will be preached in all the world as a witness unto all nations, and then shall the end come" (Matt. 24:14).

All the promises of God center in Christ, not the Jews (see Rom. 15:8–12; 2 Cor. 1:20). He, not Palestine or a Jewish nation, is the fulfillment and interpreter of all prophecy. The Israel of God is composed of people from every language, nation, and kind who place their faith in Christ as their Lord and Savior and are obedient to His Word.

Christ sends His angels to guide His faithful people. Prophecy indicates that the "everlasting gospel" is reaching its climax.

Armageddon's Glorious End

This is why the message of Revelation 14:6–12 is God's message for today. "Fear God and give glory to Him for the hour of His judgment is come...worship Him", the Creator of all.

That there is a judgment that precedes His coming is evident. How would angels know who would be "caught up to meet the Lord in the air"? How could He bring His reward with Him (see Matt. 13:30; 24:31; 1 Thess. 4:15–17; Rev. 22:12)?

Hear His words of judgment just before He comes: "Let the one who does wrong, still do wrong, let the one who is filthy, still be filthy; and let the one who is righteous still be righteous, and let the one who is holy still be holy, Behold I am coming quickly, and my reward is with me" (Rev. 22:11, 12).

"Open the gates that the righteous nation that keeps the truth—faith may enter in" (Isa. 26:2). Like Jacob in his night of wrestling, they have "prevailed." They constitute the Israel of God. Even more wonderful than being God's "chosen nation" is being the "bride" of the "Son of God". "Many will be purged, purified and refined; but the wicked will act wickedly, and none of the wicked will understand, but those who have insight will understand" (Dan. 12:10).

The Nature of the Church, Its Government, and Mission

The Nature of The Church

Wherever we turn in the New Testament, we are confronted with the church. The word occurs 115 times. In the New Testament, Christianity appears in the form of the church.

No place in Scripture is Christianity presented to us as composed of separated individuals, independent of each other, each going his own way. Such a picture does not exist in the New Testament. Christians are a unified body. They are bound together by Christ in His church.

The church is composed of people, but it is more than just a human organization. "It is nothing less than the body of Christ-- to which He gives spiritual life, and through which He manifests the fulness of His power and grace ... It is the people whom Christ has saved, in whom He dwells, to whom and through whom He reveals God (Eph. 1:22, 23)" (Augustus Strong, *Systematic Theology*, p. 888).

Note the words of Christ about His church in Matthew 16:18. Christ has a church and He built it. The church is built on Christ. Peter had just expressed his faith that Jesus was the Messiah. Peter's affirmation of faith was, "You are the Christ, the Son of the living God" (v. 16). The conviction expressed by Peter was more than a human deduction. It was more than a great human desire. The conviction expressed by Peter was more than a human conviction. This truth was from God (see v. 17). It is this belief that unites a person to Christ. It is baptism that unites the person to His people, building the church (see Acts 2:38, 41, 47).

The Lord God said, "It was not good for the man to be alone." As for Adam, so for the Son of Man. It was not good for the Son of Man to be alone. Out of His own self He brought forth His church. Without her, He was incomplete. How can Christ be any closer to His church? What can be closer than the head joined to the body?

In the New Testament, we see Christ risen, glorified, and enthroned. He is seated at the right hand of the Father, above every name; all power is His. He ministers to His church so that it might minister to the world and be built.

This is why Paul can write unbelievable statements regarding the church: "...the church, which is His body, the fulness of Him who fills all in all" (Eph. 1:22, 23). How can this be? Check out this statement: "that He might present to Himself the church in all her glory, having no spot, or wrinkle or any such thing, but that she should be holy and blameless" (5:27). How can this be?

> *As we view ourselves and others, we see many spots, wrinkles, and much blame. However, we dare say and believe these words because it is inspired truth which Christ has made possible and accomplishes in His church.*

As we view ourselves and others, we see many spots, wrinkles, and much blame. However, we dare say and believe these words because it is inspired truth which Christ has made possible and accomplishes in His church.

I. The meaning of the word.

The word "church" equates to "the Lord's house or people". "Ekklesia": The word used in the Greek NT means to, "summon forth" that which is called out. "to NT times

(Acts 19:39) ekklesia, was the designation of the assembly of the whole body of citizens in a free city-state, "called out" by the herald for the discussion and decision of public business." ... When the OT was translated into Greek about 270 B.C., the Jewish translators used the Greek word, "ekklesia" for the Hebrew word, "qahal" – congregation. (International Standard Bible Encyclopedia, vol. I, page 651.)

Jesus did not speak Greek. He spoke Aramaic. In Matthew 16:18, He no doubt used the word *qahal*. *Qahal* is translated "congregation" and "assembly" in the Old Testament. It is used for the congregation of Israel, the people of God. Jesus was saying, "I will build My congregation"—God's new Israel, His people of faith.

II. Representations or word pictures of the church.

1. "My congregation ..." "the people of God" (Matt. 16:18; 1 Pet. 2:10); "You are children of God by faith in Jesus Christ"; "Abraham's seed"; "children of Abraham" (Gal. 3:26, 7, 29).
2. "The house of God" (1 Tim. 3:15); "household of faith" (Gal. 6:10); "no more aliens, foreigners, but fellow-citizens with the saints, and of the household of God" (Eph. 2:19). Here we have the church as the family of God: The Lord is the "Householder", the Head and Provider of His family. The church is part of the "one family" of heaven and earth (Eph. 3:15).
3. "The flock of God" (Luke 12:32; Acts 20:28, 29; 1 Peter 5:2, 3).
4. "The body of Christ" (Rom. 12:5; 1 Cor. 12:12-27; Eph. 1:23; 4:4, 12, 16; 5:23, 30; Col. 1:18; 2:19).
5. The spouse of Christ (2 Cor. 11:2; Eph. 5:32).
6. The church is Christ's light in the world (Matt. 5:14; Phil. 2:15; Rev. 1:12, 20).
7. The church is the "pillar and the support of the truth" (1 Tim. 3:15). God's truth is to be seen in the church and proclaimed by the church. This figure is not that of the church resting on or being supported by the truth, but that the church itself is the monument to and support of the truth.

III. Christ's relationship to His church (Rev. 1:20; 2 and 3; 22:16)

1. The church is His love (Eph. 5:25).
2. He is the Savior of the church, His body (Eph. 5:23).
3. He is the builder of the church, the foundation, the cornerstone (1 Cor. 12:13; Matt. 21:42; Acts 4:11; Eph. 2:20; 1 Pet. 2:6, 7).
4. He is the Head of the church.
5. He is the "Good Shepherd", the "Great Shepherd", the "Chief Shepherd" (John 10:11-13; Heb. 13:20; 1 Pet. 5:4).
6. He is the "High Priest" for His people (John 14:6; 1 Tim. 2:5; Heb. 2:17; 3:1; 4:14, 15; 8:1; 9:11).

He is the "High Priest" for His people (John 14:6; 1 Timothy 2:5; Hebrews 2:17; 3:1; 4:14, 15; 8:1; 9:11). The church is "one", "one body", "one family". There should be no division. Humans make divisions. This is contrary to Christ. There should be "neither Jew no Greek..." Love for one another is the mark of His family (see John 13:35).

New Testament Church Government

The church is composed of those who have been "called out" from their lost, independent state of living into Christ. The church is a theocratic democracy. It is a society of those who are free, but are always conscious that their freedom springs from their Lord and Savior. He is Head of the church. He is their King to whom they give willing obedience.

The New Testament contains the basic "constitution" for church government. The New Testament reveals that it is the authority of Christ that was and is supreme for His church. This authority is made known by Christ's Word and the Holy Spirit.

At the same time, it was a representative government that was followed by the New Testament Church. This is evident in Acts 1:15 and 22-26. There were words in the Psalms that were applicable to Judas. "Let his office be taken by another" (Ps. 109:8). At Peter's suggestion, the believers decided to appoint someone to fill his place. After counseling together, they came up with two names on which to vote. This indicates various viewpoints. The voting may have been done by dropping pebbles of two colors into a container. Matthias was selected.

There is no suggestion that Peter or any of the apostles claimed that they had been given the power to make such appointments. The 120 believers, remembering Christ's words—"You are all brothers" (Matt. 23:8)—worked together.

When a problem arose among church members (see Acts 6), the apostles told them to "choose seven men from among yourself." There was no "kingly" authority exercised by one person making decisions for all the rest.

At the Jerusalem Council, referred to in Acts 15, we observe the same. Representatives from Antioch met with elders and believers in Jerusalem to discuss and settle a matter. In weighing the pros and cons together, they came to a corporate decision. The decision was in harmony with Scripture, prayer, and experience. They spoke of "us", "the whole church", and said, "it seemed good to the Holy Ghost and to us..." (vs. 22, 23, 25, 28). The letters they sent to the churches were not sent in the name of James, Peter, or Paul. They were sent by the authority of the whole church.

In 2 Corinthians 8:8-18, Paul speaks of the brother "who has been appointed by the churches to travel with us..." The churches had raised money for those in need and also participated in delivering it. They could report back to their churches that "all things had been done properly and in an orderly manner" (1 Cor. 14:40, NASB).

If we would remember that Christ is the Head of the church and that it is His church, not yours or mine, there would be an anxiousness to work together and minister for Him.

The Church in The End Time

The church is to be "in Christ", guided by His Word and the Holy Spirit. It is His visible witness in the world, especially in these last days (see John 15:1–5; 2 Cor. 5:17-21; 1 Cor. 12:12, 20, 28; Eph. 1:22, 23; 3:20, 21; 4:4-6; 11-13; John 14:16, 17, 26; 16:7-14; Dan. 2:28; 8:17; 12:4; 1 Tim. 4:1; 2 Tim. 2:3; 2 Peter 3:3).

The Church As Presented In Revelation

We are living in the final, Laodicean church period (see Rev. 3:14-22). We are living in the time of the sixth seal. Revelation 6:12–13 has occurred. Verses 14-17 are coming. We are living in the sealing time of Revelation 7:1-3. This sealing prepares God's people for their deliverance at Christ's appearing.

The church experienced the sweet-then-bitter experience of Revelation 10. It was brought about by widespread study of the prophecies of Daniel 7, 8, and 9. The 2,300-year prophetic time of Daniel 8:14, would end in 1843-1844. The phrase "then shall the sanctuary be cleansed" was understood to be Christ's return to earth for His people and the cleansing of the earth by fire.

Anticipating Christ's return was sweet. When it did not occur, it was bitter. Notice the last verse of Revelation 10: "You must prophecy again." God has a final message for the earth. In Revelation 12:17, Christ's church is pictured as His faithful "remnant". The dragon (Satan) wars against it to destroy it. His final attempt is pictured in Revelation 13:11-17.

God's final message—the "proclaiming again" (Rev. 10:11)—is found in Revelation 14:6-12. God's remnant church gives the appeal and warning brought by the three angels. The world faces the climax of Christ's everlasting gospel. "The hour of God's judgment is come. Worship Him who made all things". Worship Him as Creator. "Here is the patience of the saints. Here are those who keep the commandments of God and the faith of Jesus."

The keeping of God's commandments is included in the witness that the Christian faith gives to the world. Jesus said, "If you love Me you keep My commandments" (John 14:15). Observing the fourth commandment expresses our faith in God as Creator. "It is He that has made us, not we ourselves." The theory of evolution is Satan's weapon to destroy faith in God and His Word.

The church is pictured again in Revelation 14:12. It refuses to receive the "mark of the beast." It follows the example of Peter and the other apostles who answered the demands made by the Jewish rulers—"We must obey God rather than men" (Acts 5:29).

The Nature of the Church, Its Government, and Mission

The remnant continues to proclaim the call of the three angels and worship God as Creator.

Revelation 18:1-4 presents our longsuffering God as He ends His final appeal to the world. Endowed with great heavenly power, the call for "My people" to "come out of Babylon" is given. Revelation 14:14-20 pictures God's harvest, and also the world's harvest.

Revelation 15:1-4 pictures His church as standing on the sea of glass singing praises to God for all He has done. "He is righteous and true, He alone is the Holy One." The church is prominent in the marriage supper of the Lamb (see Rev. 19:7-9).

The Hierarchy of The Church Consists of Two Levels

The top level is Christ, the Head of the Church, the Scriptures, and the Holy Spirit. The second level is composed of all those who have put their faith in Christ, received the new birth, and have been baptized into Christ. All members are equal before God.

Believing this does not permit each person to do what appears right to him or her. To think that way is to replace Christ with self. It makes humans the highest authority for His church. A believer is always under Christ, the Scriptures, and the Holy Spirit. "I am not my own." Except for "the Lamb, slain from the foundation of the earth, life on earth would have ended with Adam and Eve." "In Him we live and move and have existence" (Acts 17:27, 28).

We, on the second level, know that Christ created His church. It came from Him. It is a part of Him as surely as Eve was a part of Adam. Christ continues to build His church. Using the members as His witness, He places various gifts among them. He loves His church and gave Himself for it (see Eph. 5:25). What a privilege and wonder it is to be a member!

Believers know that God has set order and gifts in the church. He is the One who has determined that "overseers" are necessary. He is the One who tells us that order and organization are needed in the church. This should be readily accepted, for human experience demonstrates that any and all accomplishments among groups require organization. There has to be a boss, coordinator, leader, captain, supervisor, call it what you will. Without such there is wasted effort, chaos, and anarchy,

Leaders are to lead. Christ gave leadership and direction to His followers. He did not tell them to go and do whatever they felt like doing. Judas is the one who would do things his own way. It is through the teaching of Scripture and gifts of the Holy Spirit that Christ leads His church.

Satan is at work to get people of ability to lead away disciples after themselves or "seize the Son's inheritance" for their own prestige and advantage. We must ever follow the example of Him who said, "I am among you as He that serves." Thank God for organization and order (see Acts 20:29, 30; Matt. 21:37–39; Luke 22:27).

Christ's Words about The Mission of The Church

"This gospel of the kingdom will be preached in all the world as a witness to all the nations, and then the end will come" (Matt. 24:14). Christ spoke these words just days before His death. Then, just as He was about to ascend to heaven, He gave what is called the Great Commission (see Matt. 28:18–20). He assured His followers of His authority, power, and presence with them. Mark 16:15, Luke 24:46–49, and John 20:31 also give emphasis to this mission. His parting words were "But you shall receive power when the Holy Spirit has come upon you; and you shall be witnesses to Me in Jerusalem, and in all Judea and Samaria, and to the end of the earth" (Acts 1:8).

This I Know—God is for Me

"But this I know that God is for me" (Psalm 56:9)

The story is told that when Napoleon was in Egypt gazing to the Sphinx, he posed a question. The sphinx has stood there for millennia. Much history has passed since it was built. In that history, we see the rise and fall of nations; what humans have accomplished; and what they have done to one another—so much tragedy and evil. The question posed was, "I wish it would tell us—is God for or against us?

God is for us! This is the record contained in the Bible's story. There are many ways this good news is presented (see John 3:16; Rom. 8:31-34). There is the original order and beauty of Creation. There is the uniqueness of humans, God's crowning act of Creation— made in His image. There is the fact that God provided the way for rebellious people to return to Him.

One institution, not often considered, which very forcefully communicates that God is for us is the Jewish legal system. It reveals that God, our Judge, is our Defender.

"In Hebrew jurisprudence every possible effort was made to save, and to protect human life because it belonged to God. The Mishna declares that: 'The Sanhedrin which so often as once in seven years condemns a man to death, is a slaughter house.' (Chandler) Dr. R. Eliezer, to quote, Greenleaf, says the Sanhedrin, 'deserves this appellation when it pronounces a like sentence once in seventy years. Benny declares that it was a maxim of the Jews that 'the Sanhedrin was to save life, not to destroy life.' (Chandler)" (Taylor G. Bunch, *Behold the Man*, pp. 66, 67).

"No court among the ancient Hebrews could consist of a single judge, Three was the number of the lowest court; three and twenty of the next highest; and seventy-one, of the Great Sanhedrin at Jerusalem. A single intelligence acting judicially would have been regarded as a usurpation of divine prerogative..."Hebrew jurisprudence provided no advocates either to defend or to prosecute. The judges were the defenders; the witnesses were the prosecutors...." (op. cit. p. 64) The Judges were for the accused. The accused were to have every benefit that the law provided. "Not under any circumstances, was a man known to be at enmity with the accused person permitted to occupy a position among the judges." (op. cit. p. 101) "Hebrew law demanded not only that every consideration possible be given to the merits of the defense, but also that every effort be made to find evidence in behalf of the defendant" (p. 105).

We see these points at work when the Scribes and Pharisees brought the woman taken in adultery to Jesus for His judgment. Their great malice rendered them unfit as witnesses. After Christ's words and writing in the sand, no witnesses remained. With no witness to condemn her, it was not for the judge to condemn her.

When God came to Adam and Eve following their disobedience, He who must judge them was for them. He clothed them. He gave them hope by His promise that One would be born into the human race and overcome the serpent, thus providing a way to "reconcile them to Himself." "God (the Judge) devises means to bring His banished home" (Gen. 3:15, 21; Heb. 2:14; 2 Cor. 5:19; 2 Sam. 14:13, 14; Rom. 8:31-39; Jere. 9:23, 29; 29:11; Psalm 118:6; 41:11; Exodus 34:5-7). This is the theme of Scripture. The Creator, Lawgiver, and Judge has provided forgiveness, redemption, and eternal life.

When God Mortgaged Heaven

Jesus was "the Lamb slain from the foundation of the world" (Rev. 13:8) and thus able to execute "the mystery which from the beginning of the world has been hid in Christ" (Eph. 3:9). "God... saved us... according to His own purpose and grace which was given us in Christ Jesus before the world began" (2 Tim. 1:9). "For our redemption heaven itself was imperiled" (E.G. White,

Christ's Object Lessons, p. 196). God's plans and promises for the reconciliation and salvation of humanity endangered heaven and God's throne.

Think about it. "The wages of sin is death." Adam and Eve should have died, thus ending the human race. On what basis could they be kept alive? How can we justify God forgiving sin, taking Enoch to heaven, and the many merciful things He did while the penalty for sin remained unpaid? In a legal sense, God must sign a promissory note. What security backed up His promise? His throne—heaven itself. Heaven was mortgaged.

Then, in the fulness of time, God sent His Son, the promised seed of the woman. Jesus, by the life He lived, defeated Satan and his claim about God's law and sin. He could have taken His perfect humanity and returned to heaven. In His humanity, he had shown that God's law is holy and Adam and Eve could and should have kept it. He had justified God, but not us. His life magnified our sinfulness and deepened our guilt. Only by taking our sin upon His perfect life, suffering and dying the death we deserve, could heaven's mortgage for our salvation be satisfied. This was the mystery hidden from the foundation of the world.

"It is finished!" When He, the Righteous One, died for us, the unrighteous, heaven's mortgage was paid. "Now salvation, and strength, and the kingdom of our God, and the power of His Christ, have come...." (Rev. 12:10). "Though there was grief among those who loved Him on earth, there was joy in heaven. Glorious to the eyes of heavenly beings was the promise of the future. A restored creation, a redeemed race, having conquered sin could never fall—this the result to flow from Christ's completed work, God and angels saw." "The day that was a day of rejoicing to all heaven, was to the disciples a day of uncertainty, confusion and perplexity" (E.G. White, *The Desire of Ages*, pp. 769, 790, 758).

Come to Christ. By His grace, you can live the wonder of His great salvation.

God on Death Row (A Meditation)

Regarding the heading above, some might say, "What a blasphemous title. How dare you write such a thing! You sound

Armageddon's Glorious End

like an atheist, a Communist." He is not now on "death row", but He was. Who placed Him there?

No one forced Him there. God the Son committed Himself to be "The Lamb slain from the foundation of the world." In heaven's council of peace, the decision was made.

Why would God place Himself in such a position? To rescue humanity. Legally, our race should have ended with Adam and Eve. They sinned and deserved death. For more than four thousand years, God stayed on death row. The continual morning and evening sacrifices in His sanctuary on earth were a constant reminder that He would be "the Lamb that was slain."

How could He stay so committed as He viewed the self-centered rebelliousness of even His chosen people? *See the idol they have placed in Your temple. They scoff at Your word. Look what they are doing to the earth that You gave to them. They have filled it with violence.* However, God could also see His people of faith—His Enochs, Abrahams, Jochebeds, Ruths, Marys, Johns, Pauls, and thousands whose names are lost to us, but not to Him. He did not fail or become discouraged. His face was set like flint and in all their afflictions, He was afflicted.

Finally, "in the fullness of time", the day came. "A body have You prepared for me"; "God sent His Son, born of a woman, born under the law that we might be given the full rights of sons."

He knew why He was in the world. His baptism by John is an example for humans, but it also symbolized the laying down of His life for the world. "Truly, truly, I say to you, except a kernel of wheat fall into the ground and die it abides alone, but if it die it brings forth much fruit...Now is my soul troubled; what shall I say? Father save me from this hour: but for this cause I have come to this hour" (John 12:24, 27).

First, He must be the Lamb without spot or blemish. He must live the life Adam and Eve could and should have lived—a life of faith that is in full conformity to God and His law. His life must show what it means to love God with all one's heart, soul, mind, and strength and love all humanity as oneself; to do justice, love mercy, and walk humbly with God. He was able to say, "I have kept my Father's commandments." "I do always those things that please Him." "Which of you convicts me of sin?" Pilates verdict—"I find no fault in Him"—stands, for it echoed the verdict of the divine righteousness of all heaven.

The Lamb of God, on death row, took upon Himself the sin of the world, that righteousness might prevail in place of the anarchy which we have on earth. He who knew no sin became sin for us. He, the Righteous One, died for us, the unrighteous ones. He gives us eternal life. "O come let us worship and bow down. Let us kneel before the Lord our Maker."

Speaking as a Serpent

"And I saw another beast coming up out of the earth; and he had two horns like a lamb, and he spoke as the [serpent]" (Rev. 13:11). Does this version change the meaning of the verse, or does it better reflect what the Lord had in mind in giving Revelation to John? Researching the word "dragon" suggested this change. The *Encyclopedia of Religions* article, "Dragon", states, "The word points to serpents. The Greek term means, serpent'" (pp. 2430, 2431). In Exodus 7:9–12, the Hebrew word rendered as "serpent" is *tannin* and is most often translated as "dragon". Revelation 12:9 and 20:2 use both "dragon" and "serpent" as designations for Satan. Isaiah 27:1 refers to "Leviathan", "serpent", and "dragon" in an interchangeable manner. *Webster's Collegiate Dictionary*, fifth edition and *Webster's New World College Dictionary* both give "serpent" as a meaning for "dragon".

This beast in Revelation 13:11, "having two horns like a lamb and speaking as the serpent", is lying. In Revelation 16:13, 19:20, and 20:10, he is labeled "the false prophet." Satan uses it to "deceive the whole world" (12:9).

This beast had "two horns like a lamb". Twenty-eight times in the book of Revelation, the word "lamb" is used in reference to Christ. This one time the word "lamb" is used to refer to the horns of this beast. This beast has Christian characteristics. This false prophet is "a wolf in sheep's clothing." It claims to speak for Christ. In that the horns are a symbol of power, the signs and wonders performed are claimed to be evidence of the power of Christ. The miracles are regarded as heavenly power, "fire from heaven" (13:13).

Armageddon's Glorious End

In Eden, the serpent's words contradicted God's word. Thus, in this final conflict, the worship required by the two beasts of Revelation 13 is in contradiction to God's Word as He has given it in the Bible (the "dragon" or serpent is found in many religions and cultures. It symbolized "forces—elements that interfered with the correct order and functioning of the world." The dragon was the cause of evil. There are legends of gods or people who sought to destroy "the primeval chaotic dragon." These reflect God's original promise that one would be born into the human race who would "crush the serpent's head" and "destroy him that had the power of death, that is the devil") (Gen. 3:15; Heb. 2:14).

"Ancient writings depict a war between the gods and a dragon of chaos (abyss)." They also refer to an evil seven-headed dragon (See *Seventh-day Adventist Bible Commentary*, vol. 4, on Isaiah 27:1; and vol. 8, p. 668, article, "Leviathan").

Why Would a Christian Worship on Saturday?

For fifteen years we lived in New Jersey. Occasionally a question would come. It was, "Why would a Christian worship on Saturday? I thought only Jews worshiped on Saturday." My answer was, "Because of my Savior, Jesus."

One Sabbath, a controversy arose because of what His disciples were doing. Jesus replied, "The Sabbath was made for man and not man for the Sabbath. Therefore the Son of Man is lord also of the Sabbath" (Mark 2:27, 28). Think about these words.

He said, "The Sabbath was *made*". When was it made? One has only to read the first thirty-four verses of the Bible to discover when it was made. It, like marriage, comes to us from Creation. It was part of the perfection of Eden. It was not a shadow of anything. It is the memorial to our Creator God—Father, Son, and Holy Spirit.

Who made it? The Lord Himself made it. He made it by His acts. He rested from His work of Creation. He made it by His words. He sanctified it—set it apart—declared it holy (Gen. 2:1–3).

Why was it made? Christ said, "it was made *for man*". It was a gift for the human race. Just as Adam and Eve were made for each other and as Eden and all it contained was made for the benefit of Adam, Eve, and their descendants, so the Sabbath was made for the blessing of all people.

The Sabbath was to be a day of joyful celebration with their Creator. Humans, created in the image of God, were the crowning act of His Creation. Adam and Eve needed to keep connected to

Him. They were surrounded by all the wonders and beauty of the new creation. They could think and be free to act. There was so much to see, experience, and learn. In such brilliant conditions, it would be so easy to make the things of nature and their interests the center of their lives.

Only by staying united with their Creator could they become all that God intended for them. Only by staying united with God could they keep living. Separation from God leads to self-centered living. That results in evil, decay, and death.

Resting in God every seventh day was God's way to keep them holy. It is Jesus Christ who is "Lord of the Sabbath." He, not the Pharisees, teaches us its meaning and how to "Remember" and "keep it holy." Jewish teachers had added hundreds of rules about what was and wasn't permissible to do on the Sabbath. The Sabbath was presented as something that we do for God to get salvation. One Jewish teacher wrote that if the nation as a whole would perfectly keep the Sabbath, the Messiah would come.

Jesus And The Sabbath

On the Sabbath, it was the custom of Jesus to: 1. Meet with His people. 2. Teach the people. 3. Perform miracles. Seven Sabbath miracles are recorded. The idea that the Sabbath was given for the good of humanity is the thought that Jesus made prominent in His ministry.

It is still the same. Christ, in a special way, meets with His people on His holy day. By His vicar, the Holy Spirit, He teaches them as they study the Scripture. He still works the miracle of changed lives as people "Remember the Sabbath day to keep it holy" and worship Him in faith.

There were Sabbaths that were later given to Israel: Passover, Pentecost, Day of Atonement, etc. They came after sin came into the world. They were "shadow" Sabbaths in that they shadowed forth the work that Christ would do in redeeming humans and restoring the lost creation. They were "against us" in that they were a reminder of man's fallen condition with the death sentence over him. The Creation Sabbath was a gift *for* man. God pronounced a blessing on it. It was never against us.

Why Would a Christian Worship on Saturday?

It is the life, death, and resurrection of Christ that provides escape from sin and death. "For by grace you have been saved through faith, and that not of yourselves; it is the gift of God. Not of works lest anyone should boast. For we are His workmanship, created in Christ Jesus for good works, which God prepared beforehand that we should walk in them" (Eph. 2:8–10). Keeping God's Sabbath is one of the "good works" which God prepared and gave to people. "If you love Me you keep My Commandments" (John 14:15). Christians keep the Sabbath because of their love for their Savior.

Another impressive thought to consider is, 'Why has Satan put forth such immense efforts to discredit and destroy God's holy seventh day?' He "makes war against those who keep the commandments..." (Rev. 12:17). His first effort was to have the day forgotten. God says, "Remember". Then Satan discredited it by having hundreds of regulations added to it, making it a burdensome yoke. Messiah corrected that. The old serpent has successfully worked to replace Sabbath observance with Sunday observance. His teaching that grace does away with obedience is widely accepted. His continuing efforts against God's Sabbath are because he knows its importance and the great blessings it brings to people.

It is the life, death, and resurrection of Christ that provides escape from sin and death.

The words "let no man judge you in respect of a sabbath day" are right. The Lord alone is Judge. All will answer to Him for what they have done with Jesus and His gift of the Sabbath. His Law, not a human law, instructs our worship.

The shadow sabbaths are fulfilled in Christ. "Christ is our Passover" (1 Cor. 5:7). The risen Christ, still bearing His perfect humanity, is the "first fruits" of all who are resurrected to eternal life (1 Cor. 15:20–23). The life and death of God's Messiah would "make the law great and glorious" (Isaiah 42:21). Therefore, Paul wrote, "the law is holy, and the commandment is holy, righteous, and good...it is spiritual."

As Christ died on the cross, He cried, "It is finished!" An earthquake split the veil of the temple and opened graves. His perfect life and death in our place provided salvation. It ratified His new covenant. He was laid in a tomb where He rested. His Sabbath rest in the grave was parallel to His (God's) rest on the seventh day of Creation. A work had been finished. He is the "ladder", the Way, the Truth, and the Life, by which fallen humans can come to God. "God was in Messiah, reconciling the world unto Himself."

His death tore off the gate of death and left it there on Calvary's hill. In heaven, that Sabbath was a day of rejoicing. All of God's promises were sealed for fulfillment. Heaven waited in joyous expectation for the "third day" to arrive.

Early in the first day, "while it was yet dark, there was another earthquake as an angel descended, rolled back the stone that covered the entrance to the tomb." Imagine the scene. Hear the angel say, "Your Father calls you." Picture Jesus walking out. The folded grave clothes left in the tomb show He is in charge.

His resurrection proclaimed His victory. The memorial of His resurrection is not a day. The memorial to His resurrection is His church—His people. Seven times in the book of Acts, his disciples say, "We are witness to His resurrection." The life they lived and words they spoke witnessed to their risen Lord. Christians are baptized into His death and raised to walk in newness of life. It is living a new life in Christ 365 days a year that is the true memorial to His resurrection. It insults Him if we live like Mardi Gras most of the year and then for one day, or forty days, deny ourselves some pleasure for His sake. Christ gave no command to honor Sunday. The teaching and example of Jesus are the reasons Christians worship the Creator and Redeemer on His seventh-day Sabbath.

Bibliography

Anderson, R.A. *Unfolding Daniel's Prophecies*. Nampa, ID: Pacific Press Publishing Association.

Anderson, R.A. *Unfolding the Revelation*. Nampa, ID: Pacific Press Publishing Association.

Bunch, Taylor G., *Behold the Man*. Nashville, TN: Southern Publishing Association.

Buttrick, George A. *Interpreter's Dictionary of The Bible*. Nashville, TN: Abingdon Press.

Froom, Le Roy E. *The Prophetic Faith of Our Fathers*. Hagerstown, MD: Review and Herald Publishing Association.

Lenski, R.C.H. *The Interpretation of St. John's Revelation*.

Maxwell, C. Mervyn, *God Cares*. Nampa, ID: Pacific Press Publishing Association.

Neufeld, Don and Julia Neuffer, eds. *Seventh-day Adventist Bible Students Source Book, Commentary Reference Series*. Hagerstown, MD: Review and Herald Publishing Association.

Nichols, F.D., ed. *Seventh-day Adventist Bible Commentary*. Hagerstown, MD: Review and Herald Publishing Association.

Read, W.E. "The War of Armageddon." *Review and Herald* 131, no. 11 (March 18, 1954): 7.

Shea, William H. *Daniel: A Reader's Guide*. Nampa, ID: Pacific Press Publishing Association.

Silver, Abba Hillel. *A History of Messianic Speculation in Israel*. Boston, MA: Beacon Press.

Smith, Uriah. *Daniel and the Revelation*. Hagerstown, MD: Review and Herald Publishing Association.

Smith, William Taylor. *International Standard Bible Encyclopedia*. Chicago, IL: The Howard-Severance Company.

Strong, Augustus. *Systematic Theology*. Philadelphia, PA: American Baptist Publication Society. Public Domain.

White, Ellen G. *The Acts of the Apostles*. Mountain View, CA: Pacific Press Publishing Association, 1911.

White, Ellen G. *Christ Triumphant*. Hagerstown, MD: Review and Herald Publishing Association, 1999.

White, Ellen G. *Christ's Object Lessons*. Washington, DC: Review and Herald Publishing Association, 1900.

White, Ellen G. *The Desire of Ages*. Mountain View, CA: Pacific Press Publishing Association, 1898.

White, Ellen G. *Education*. Mountain View, CA: Pacific Press Publishing Association, 1903.

White, Ellen G. *The Great Controversy*. Mountain View, CA: Pacific Press Publishing Association, 1911.

Encyclopedia of Religions.
Webster's Collegiate Dictionary.
Webster's New World College Dictionary.
World Book Encyclopedia.
Webster's New College Dictionary.
Catechism of The Catholic Church.
The Restoration of The Gospel of Jesus Christ
Journal of The Adventist Theological Society.

TEACH Services, Inc.
P U B L I S H I N G

We invite you to view the complete
selection of titles we publish at:
www.TEACHServices.com

We encourage you to write us
with your thoughts about this,
or any other book we publish at:
info@TEACHServices.com

TEACH Services' titles may be purchased in
bulk quantities for educational, fund-raising,
business, or promotional use.
bulksales@TEACHServices.com

Finally, if you are interested in seeing
your own book in print, please contact us at:
publishing@TEACHServices.com
We are happy to review your manuscript at no charge.

www.ingramcontent.com/pod-product-compliance
Lightning Source LLC
Chambersburg PA
CBHW070550160426
43199CB00014B/2451